Love After Abuse

9 Survivors' Stories Of Finding Love After Abuse

Copyright © 2020 by Lisa Nicole Publishing

All rights reserved. This book or any portion thereof may not be reproduced or used in any manner whatsoever without the express written permission of the publisher except for the use of brief quotations in a book review.

Printed in the United States of America

ISBN: 9798652883270

Dedication

This book is dedicated to Karen Bobbitt, Harley Dree, Alivia Ferreira, Heather Graham, Carmeletta Joseph, Sarah Mitchell, Shanda Roberts and Hadassah Shalom. Thank you for trusting me to help share your story.

You ladies are amazing and strong and brave and beautiful. Watching you journey through this and grow and find your voice through writing and sharing your story has been an honor. Your bravery and resilience can be seen throughout your chapters and in the life that you have created for yourself today.

Thank you for your vulnerability and willingness to share your story in an effort to not just free yourself but to free others. I have no doubt that there will be lives saved because of you sharing your story.

CONTENTS

Introduction 9

Lisa Alexander M.S. 10

Carmaletta Joseph 22

Heather Kathleen Graham.. 28

Shanda Roberts... 40

Hadassah Shalon... 50

Karen Martin Bobbitt.. 62

Harley Dree 84

Sarah Mitchell 109

Alivia Ferreira 124

Acknowledgement
By Authors:

Lisa Alexander: God thank you for loving me enough to keep me even when I didn't want to be kept. Thank you to my husband Hosea, for showing me the best love ever, I love you so much. For telling me that I can do anything, actually believing that I can and supporting me as I seek to conquer all God has called me to. Thank you to my 3 children Ahriel, Ezera and Joy for sacrificing time with me while I pursue my passions and work in service to others, I aim to make you proud. To my parents for showing me Jesus, you could have given me no greater gift, I love you.

Sarah Mitchell: Above all, I thank God Almighty, who brought me out of the darkness I was in, and into being a survivor, from nights of hour long prayers, to no words just tears streaming down my face, He knew exactly what I needed, when I needed it, and was NEVER a second late. Second, my sister, Julie, and her family, for giving my family a safe place to call home when needed. Third, my best friends who pulled me through and listened when needed, no matter what time. My son, Jeremiah, for giving me strength and a reason to keep moving forward. Safe Haven of Tarrant County, for all the guidance and recovery you provide me and other women in need. Lisa, for this amazing opportunity to show other women there is hope and love on the other side. And to my current boyfriend, Donny, for showing me and reminding me daily of the love I deserve, despite my past.

Heather Graham: First, and most importantly, I would like to thank my daughter, Jessica, who was the driving force behind me participating in this collaboration, and who has always been one of my biggest supporters and closest friends. Thank you to my boys, Nicholas and Timothy, who are my rocks and are always there to love and protect their family. Special thanks to my parents, Alan and Barbara, who were there to support all of us with unconditional love in our darkest hours, and have been there time and time again in the days, months and years that followed. Finally, a life time of love and thanks to my soul mate and best friend, Michael, who has shown me the true meaning of love and commitment, taught me to believe in happily ever after, helped me learn that life really is about the journey, not the destination, and was the vital piece that finally completely made our family whole.

Alivia Ferreira: This is my dedication to all those who are suffering and surviving domestic violence. We are warriors. Thank you to my mother, grandparents and my best friend Tyler for being the best support systems out there and pushing me to get where I am today.

Shanda Roberts: I would like to thank my Lord & Saviour Jesus Christ for giving me the willpower to walk away...FOR GOOD! I also want to thank Lisa Alexander giving us an opportunity to tell our stories. Thank you to the P2P team also my sisters. Blood couldn't make us any closer. Last but not least, I would love to thank my family. My loving husband George and my beautiful children for always supporting me.

Carmeletta Josepha: I want to acknowledge my support system. My Husband for putting up with my crazy days and knowing exactly what to say. My children for understanding that Mom does everything to make sure they're taken cared of to my best ability. I know Mommy stays on the run, but it's all for the best. My Mother for always being a shoulder to lean on when I just need a minute and my siblings for knowing exactly when to make me laugh

Harley Dee: Thank YOU, for picking up this book seeking courage, healing, or even the obtaining of knowledge to help others on your life's path. Special recognition from my journey has been more than earned by: One to One Women Coaching Women, Give an Hour, the founders of Door to Serenity, Ms. Susan, the Sawyers, Dr. Hughes, M.D.H., and of course T+F.

Hadassah Shalom: "I would like to acknowledge the Creator of the Universe and my family for guiding my steps. In the darkest of times they remain my light and my shield. I would also like to thank my friends Lisa Alexander, Lecia Gray, and Mark Smiley for always encouraging me to explore my writing talent...here is to living, loving, and writing!

Karen Bobbitt

Thank you to everyone who saw me through the past eight years, it was a wild ride indeed. If I could go back, knowing what I know now, I would not change a thing. Every experience: good, bad and ugly; played a part in making me who I am today. Besides, without all of that I never would have found the most kind and loving husband a woman could want, and I would not trade Steve for the world. Smooches.

Introduction

Thank you for taking the time to pick up this book. Whether you are a victim, survivor or supporter of a survivor just know that you are getting ready to read stories that will open your eyes to the world of domestic abuse. Not only that, but you are going to read triumphant stories of women who decided that they were no longer going to accept anything less than what they deserved.

I encourage you to share these stories, and this book. Someone you know and love is experiencing domestic violence and silence hides violence. These pages are filled with the stories of women who have said no more, it's time to Stand Up.

It's one thing to go through traumatic experiences, but it's another to share those experiences with others. The vulnerability on these pages is nothing short of amazing. May you be enlightened and empowered as you read.

Lisa Alexander M.S.

Founder and Executive Director of Stand Up Survivor Inc.

www.facebook.com./standupsurvivor

www.instagram.com/standupsurvivor

www.standupsurvivor.com

lisa@standupsurvivor.com

lisanicolealexander@yahoo.com

Lisa Alexander is the founder of Stand Up Survivor, a 501 c (3) non-profit organization created to educate and bring awareness of domestic violence. Her focus is to educate, empower and equip those who are survivors as well as the community, organizations, churches and schools.

Through this organization she understands the importance of meeting individuals where they are and helping them see a future, they may have never thought possible.

Lisa Alexander holds a Bachelor's in Psychology, a Master's in Counseling Psychology and is currently a Doctoral candidate focusing her dissertation on domestic violence and the church.

Lisa has spoken locally and internationally to groups, churches, radio and news stations. She is also an author where she shares her story of domestic violence and how you can not only survive but thrive.

As a survivor, she chooses to Stand Up and use her voice to help as many women as possible find theirs.

Her motto is...*until every woman is free.*

Lisa Alexander

I wanted love, the love that I had to give.
I wanted to wake up with the same person every day.
I wanted to go to sleep in safety and wake up in peace.
I wanted to be in a healthy relationship.
I wanted to love and be loved.

I met my abuser at 19, married him at 23 and stayed for 6 years. During our relationship I experienced all types of abuse. Physical, financial, sexual and emotional, psychological. But I loved my ex-husband, didn't believe in divorce and we had two children. I really wanted my marriage to work. I didn't want to embarrass my family and I didn't want to fail. I wanted my children to live in a household with both of their parents. I remember feeling so lost, so hurt so confused and so very, very sad. But in the midst of those feelings I also felt like I couldn't take any more of the pain that I was enduring. I literally wanted to die. I slowly began to realize that this abuse was going to literally kill me, and I decided that I needed to find a way to finally be free.

And free I did get. And as I write this I feel as free as a bird. But you need to know that this journey that I'm on has not been easy, and still isn't. But I needed to start down the road so that I could eventually get to the point that I could even be writing in this book about finding life and love after abuse. I had to take that first step, and that was all on ME.

Shortly after I got divorced I met someone. He was a wonderful man and the year we were together was great, while it ended hard I learned so much through it. I learned that I was worthy of being loved. I learned that there were so many great qualities about myself and learned about the normalcies of a relationship. During this time I was a single mom, going to school full time and working full time. I had full time bills and full time responsibilities. Yet, I was still hoping and searching for love. I wasn't willing to give up on my happily ever after. You may wonder why I included this fact in the book. See just because it didn't work out right away with someone I met after abuse, I still learned, I still grew, and I still needed that season in my life.

Because I had met my ex-husband at such a young age I realized that I had never really dated. So that's one thing I did do, was date. There were seasons where I didn't date anyone and focused on one thing or the other. But as my friend Rachel would tell you, I was not afraid to date. I also learned that I had a "type" of guy that I was attracted to. And while some would say it was similar to my ex-husband I would say they were similar to my daddy, my first love. A handsome, black man with a beard and a belly! I laugh at that now, but it's true. I had a type and I usually dated men that only looked like that.

While dating I learned that it was ok to be picky. I prayed about it a lot and asked God that if that person was not for me to not let me waste any time with them. I truly wanted Gods will for my life and nothing less. Although during that 6 year time frame of being divorced to being remarried I was lonely, there wasn't much in me that was willing to settle for just anything. I knew that I had literally crawled out of hell and there was nothing inside of me that was willing to settle for even a glimpse of anything similar.

I knew what I wanted, I knew what I had to offer and most of all I knew who I was. Now don't get me wrong…all of that did not come overnight. It came from attempts and failures. It came from ups and downs. It came from therapy and experiences, lots of failed ones too.

Now my chapter is not to tell you that I have figured out life and love, because I definitely haven't. But my chapter is meant to give you hope and let you know that there is hope for you too. My husband and I are coming up on our four year anniversary. I guess it's true when they say time flies when you're having fun. It feels like it was just yesterday that we met. I can't believe that it's already been 4 years. But here is a bit on our story….

I was working for Orange County Public Schools downtown at the district office as a resource teacher assisting homeless families. I'd been there for 3 years when I was told I needed to take a test to keep my position. Well I took the 4 part test and failed the math portion. I actually failed the math portion 3 times! At over $200 a test to retake I wasn't willing to continue to take this test. Not only was math my toughest subject, but I also realized that if I was going to invest in something it needed to be something that I was passionate about. And while I loved my job, those I worked with and those we served, I knew that it was not my passion. After failing this test I decided it was time for me to do something new.

One thing about me is that I have never been afraid to pick up and move, relocate, or try something new. When I was 17 I went to China for the first time with a group. I went 3 times after that on my own and stayed there each time for a significant amount of time. So relocating for me was not a big deal.

But my mom will tell you...one thing about me...is I will go anywhere...but my kids are coming with me. I will put them in my pocket or back pack and go. We were a trio the 3 of us. My kids and I went though the best of times and the worst of times together. I am thankful that most of it they have no recollection of, so they say, but it was all about the 3 of us. I lived and breathed for my children. It was important for ME to be OK because then I knew then, that THEY would be ok.

So I started looking for jobs and decided that I would take the one I liked no matter where it was. Well it happened to be in Clearwater, FL. I packed my kids up, moved into an apartment for only $99 and we were on our way. Moving there was the best decision ever! We were close to the beach, close but not too close to family and finally I felt like I could finally breathe. There were no expectations from anyone or any additional stressors. The only issue was, while I was loving it we actually moved CLOSER to my ex-husband, which meant, uh o, he may want to execute his rights from the parental plan and see my kids. See ever since we got divorce he has NEVER complied with the parenting plan and I've basically parented alone 99% of the time. While this was a fear of mine i didn't let it stop me.

I decided after being there for about 6 months that I would try online dating. I have to add that I met the most amazing woman named Kate. She is a key part of my story during this season of my life. See, God always placed people in my life along my journey that He knew I would need and would help me get through every season.

She had recently moved to Clearwater from New Jersey for the same position I was in. She walked in one day, new to our staff meeting and I thought, O, I hope we can be friends! And soon enough we were inseparable. She became a lifeline for me there. She loved my children and they loved her. She was beautiful, kind hearted, thoughtful. All of the things I needed and wanted in a friend especially in this season of my life. My kids thought she was the best person EVER and we did everything together! We even decided to try and do online dating together too. So I put a profile on POF- plenty of fish. It was interesting to say the least. I had gone on a few dates, got catfished a time or two, but overall nothing great. I had decided to take my picture down and just from time to time check out guys who fit what I was looking for. And right before I was about to delete my profile I messaged this guy and he responds. He was finnneee yall. I was thinking, he is just my type! One thing we did was video chat for a while first before we ever went on our first date. He was just as handsome on video. And of course when he saw me he was happy too (I'll put that part of the story in there for him)

Anyway, in order to not make this too long....we finally met face to face in March of 2016. He lived 4 hours away in West Palm Beach. See, im not from Florida and I thought he was near where I lived, boy was I wrong. So for the next 5 months we arranged to meet up with each other. By December of 2016 we were married! Yes, 10 months later we got married. I'm sure that everyone thought I must be crazy. But by that time my parents and siblings had met him, and he asked my dad for my hand in marriage and he gave his blessing.

Our wedding was on a Friday night, simple, with just a handful of some of the most precious people in my life that had helped me along my journey. My mom, a pastor, married us. It was a day filled with so many tears of joy. I truly never thought that that day would come for me. My heart was so full.

My husband loves me so well. He has always opened my door, he always cooks (I don't cook, its overrated lol), he is a gentleman and he loves my kids as if they were his own. My daughter started calling him dad even before we got married and my son shortly after. I remember having the conversation with them about that, like are you sure? And they said mom, he's our dad, he's there for us. He is selfless when it comes to caring for his family, he is always putting us first, providing for us and making sure that we feel safe and secure.

There is nothing that I can tell him that I want or desire to do that he won't try or make happen. He's my person. He's my missing puzzle piece. We have never had to force our connection. We have always just fit. My husband has loved away ever scar that was left back from my ex-husband and continues to do so to this day. He loves me in a way I've never been loved before. I feel seen in a way I never have before, he sees me.

One thing that my husband will tell you is that I am headstrong. I don't allow him or anyone to talk to me any kind of way, to raise their voice at me or use profanity with me. He would say you don't just accept anything. See, I had made a decision in my mind to never again let anyone mistreat me in ANY way. My husband celebrates me. He pushes me. He supports me. NO matter what it is I want to do, he says you should totally do that. No matter how huge or how small he tells me to conquer the world every day.

Now don't' get me wrong our marriage is not perfect. Having dated and gotten married within such a short amount of time we have had to get to know each other while married and that can be significantly challenging. But today it's still true as the day I married him, he's amazing, he's my guy and I love him totally and completely. The best part of that is that I am loved totally and completely too.

I remember years ago asking God to please let me experience real love, a real marriage, the way that HE had designed it to be. And God has blessed me with that. In Dec 2017 we had a baby and we named her Joy. When we got married we had said we weren't going to have kids. We were good as he as children as well, grandchildren even. But I got baby fever and then comes the Joy of all of our lives. Therefore, I also got the gift of a healthy pregnancy. Both of my previous pregnancies had been filled with such abuse I didn't think want to live through them.

While our life has not been perfect, it has been good, so very good. I am so thankful and humbled every time I wake up and I see this big handsome man next to me. He's my friend, my lover and my man. He makes me feel safe and protected and I don't ever think for one moment that he would ever hurt me or my children. That feeling is priceless. My husband loves me and he loves me well. I used to dream about the love that he gives me and thank God that I get to experience it every day. I am not lucky I am blessed, so very blessed.

That feeling is one that only someone who has survived abuse can understand and truly feel deep inside. See I found Lisa after abuse and in the midst of finding Lisa, I found Love. Lisa is compiled of now 3 children, Stand Up Survivor Inc, ministry, family and Love. While navigating my way through life, God blessed me the opportunity to every day be able to live in Love. The love from Him, the love from my husband and the love from my children and family. Every day I get to help countless women, men and children that are experiencing abuse through my organization. I refuse to be silent so anyone can feel comfortable. I know that you, deserve to know that hope.

I want you, yes you reading this chapter, this book to know that you are loved. That you are deserving of love. That you are deserving of a life that allows you to truly live, breathe, be at peace and smile. A deep smile, the kind that starts on the inside and ends on your face. And I pray that you find it.

Carmaletta Joseph

Fb: Drowning In Silence

IG: @drowninginsilencedv

Twitter: @drowninginsilencedv

Email: drowninginsilencedv@yahoo.com

Carmeletta is a ten year survivor of Domestic violence. She is a loving wife of nine years to her now husband and dedicated mother of four children. She graduated in 2005 from Washington Marion High School where she received her Certified Nursing Assist Certificate. She is a 2010 graduate of Unitech Training Academy where she received her certification in Phlebotomy and EKG Tech. She is a co-teacher at CPSB where Carmeletta earned her CDA (Child Development Associate) and Ancillary Teaching Certificate. She is the Author of *"Drowning in Silence"*, an autobiography about the six year domestic violence relationship she was in and how she found her way out. She is a Domestic Abuse Advocate, Louisiana Coalition Against Domestic Violence Member, and the President of No More Drowning in Silence Organization. Along with her board, they aim to reach out to domestic violence victims and their families throughout the year. Carmeletta is a member of the BAYOUFOUR, where she and three other beautiful inspirational authors are bonded for the purpose of healing others' brokenness through their own brokenness. They share personal stories of domestic violence, self-love, self-care, sexual abuse, gun violence, and grief.

Carmaletta Joseph

So here I am... I have left what I knew was life and trying to figure out my next steps. With two small baby girls, ages three and two months old. I had no vehicle, struggling through college, and still trying to work a full time job. The strain of life was pushing me into a dark hole that I was screaming to not go into. How could I? I had just stepped away from what I thought was total darkness and evil. Yet, falling into my own self-made trap of hell. My mother always came through with support for us. Because I was going to work and back even with my late nights and as for school, I just gave up. There was no way I could juggle it with everything I had going on. I was trying to find ways to soothe the hurt, pain, depression, and feeling of loneliness. I went through moments of thinking, I just needed fast money and even thought about stripping. It was the fastest way to get what I wanted and needed at that time. Thank God that plan never came into play! I was working at a local grocery store and had been watching a fellow employee there. He was so sweet to me and very respectful to the fact that I was in a relationship. Yet, soon as that fell apart and I sought the chance to move on. Though it was quick, I knew there was something about this guy that was special. I would like to say that first hug said a thousand words and gave me more comfort than anyone ever in my life. He was there and treated my girls with as much respect as he treated me with. He took on a cold heart and it warmed again in ways I still cannot believe. Remember, your victories often come through your valleys.

I started dating this new guy and had not yet gotten over all of the hurt I had recently endured. Lord, I do not know how he took me in with so much grace. I was rough around the edges and my heart was set on zero degrees. The simplest thing set me off into an," I don't give a damn moment". I had my guards up and that wall in front of my soul was built up with stones, bricks, wood, and nails. There was no way I was letting anyone get as close as I had once let my abuser. My anger was at an all-time high. Many times I was asked why I was so cold hearted. No matter what, my new boyfriend was determined to get through it. As he would say," Blind, crippled, or crazy...We're gone make it". He was willing to meet me at that wall with every tool he needed to get through to my soul and show me real love.

As crazy as it was and the many trails he had to go through, that wall came falling down. Giving him just enough space to walk through. He got though and I thank God that he did. I still was dealing with those left over bricks surrounding that space. Every brick left over, carried their on burdens. From pain to excitement and even down to depression. I realized this was something I had to deal with and strive every day to continue on my life journey. Day and night I worried. Was my ex going to come back and kill me, was he watching me as I visited my family, was there any kind of way that he could have gotten into my home to set up a camera, or even been waiting in one of the dark closets. See, I had stayed in my same apartment and I could see the haunting revisal of abuse happening repeatedly in my head. The nightmares kept me up all night. Though no one was there some nights, I heard his voice. It was as if I could hear him breathing in my sleep and could even smell the strong smell of marijuana. Waking up in deep sweats and heavy breathing became normal for me. There was nights that my then, new boyfriend found me laying on the couch at night because, I was scared to sleep in my room. I did not like the idea of doors being opened in my room while I slept at night. I can honestly say now, I still do not. Call me crazy but, nights I woke up in panic seeing his dark shadow coming from there. I lived in an apartment complex that did not have washer and dryer hookups within the home. The thought of going downstairs and across the driveway made my anxiety, which I did not know at that time what it was, hit an all-time high. Not knowing if he was in there waiting.

Physically I moved on but, mentally my mind was buried six feet under in my past with stones, barbwire, bricks, and chains layered over it. I built up the strength to move from my haunting apartment. It was months down the road and I was ready to start life with my new boo. I knew this was the guy for me. My family loved him, my girls was spoiled behind him, and Mommy was astonished at all of the positivity that came from this new man. Here we were, moved into our new home, in a new little city right out of Lake Charles, and newly engaged. Yes guys, he had then proposed. Though still working in Lake Charles we traveled and took great pride in our relationship and new beginning. The long road was not over for myself due to past life I had then lived with my abuser but, I was happy. Many days I sat in court going back and forth over a custody battle and child support. Finally, things were set. I had my someone there to support, love, and soothe my mindset through my darkest times. He loved me unconditionally and vowed to never set me on the same path of destruction as I had been once before. It was only through trusting God that I knew this love would last forever.

Heather Kathleen Graham

www.hkgraham.com

hgraham416@gmail.com

www.facebook.com/hkgraham1

www.instagram.com/hkg41670

www.twitter.com/Heather41670

Heather Kathleen Graham is an avid writer and entrepreneur who successfully built several direct sales businesses over the last 20 years. She led a team of over 200 consultants, earning awards for top personal and team sales multiple years in a row. In 2014, she helped develop and run a start-up non-profit organization, Victory For Vets Inc., whose mission is to raise awareness in the community of the needs of local Veterans that suffer from the effects of military related Post Traumatic Stress along with funds to provide service dogs and training for Veterans. She was responsible for forming a partnership with several local organizations to create a Veteran Service Dog Program and currently is running the program.

Heather lives in Central New York with her fiancé Mike. They have 6 incredible children – Nicholas, Jessica, Timothy, Melissa, Amanda & Kristina and three amazing grandchildren – Jacob, Emma and Ethan. Heather is currently fulfilling her dreams as both a writer and freelance marketer. She enjoys traveling, golf, sports and spending time with her family and friends.

Rise From The Ashes
Heather Graham

Just as the majestic Phoenix dies in a burst of flames only to rise up from its own ashes and be born again, she rises up from the depths of pain and despair, a new creature, with not just the ability to once again love herself, but to also be loved.

It's easy to believe in fairytales when you are young and naïve. Happily ever after, a knight in shining armor galloping in and sweeping you off your feet – rescuing you from everything you think is 'wrong' with your life. In the early summer of 1989, I was nineteen years old and had just finished my first year of college. My summer began with an ugly breakup with a boy from school. Around that time, I met "him". The man that would offer me everything I thought I ever wanted, while at the same time destroying everything I ever knew or believed about myself. When you are young and naïve, it is easy to ignore the warning signs, to pretend everything is ok, to believe it will get better. Three months after I met "him", I was pregnant, and then married, and had a miscarriage – all before I was twenty years old. Within that short period of time I already knew that I had made the biggest mistake of my life. You see, the control, isolation, manipulation and abuse had already begun. It was subtle, for sure, but looking back, I can see it clearly now. At that time, I didn't know how to get out, I didn't know how to say, "I was wrong, this isn't what I want". How do you face being married and divorced in less than a year? How do you tell your family "I want to come home"?

So I stayed – hoping and praying it would get better. It did not. Oh there were times, moments, even days, where to the outside world, and even in my mind, I was the luckiest girl in the world. An adoring husband who put me on a pedestal and showered me with love and gifts, three beautiful children who were smart, healthy and happy and never wanted for anything. And in reality, to the outside world, that was exactly what we had. But behind closed doors, hidden away from prying eyes, that was nowhere even close to what we lived.

Twenty years of verbal, emotional and physical abuse at the hands of a monster who controlled and manipulated his family all in the name of 'love'. Abuse that escalated over the years because of a worsening drug and alcohol problem that catapulted our family into a never ending nightmare we could not escape.

By the spring of 2009, 'he' had begun to lose his ability to hide who he truly was from others. No longer was there a façade when we were in the public eye and 'he' would explode in a frightening rage in front of neighbors, family, friends and strangers alike.

But afterwards, it was always my fault. I made him lose his temper; I said something wrong, did something wrong, ignored him, didn't care about him or support him. It all ended on a warm summer night in June. Our oldest son graduated from high school.

What should have been one of the happiest days of our lives became a day that I wish I could not remember. He raged in front of family and friends, growing increasingly volatile throughout the day and then went to bed. The relief we all felt was heavy in the air – you could actually feel it. But I was afraid. I've always trusted my instincts – that feeling in the pit of your stomach, female intuition, call it what you like. It was as if deep in my soul I knew that this was going to be the end – that something was going to happen. I was afraid. My parents had come from California to watch their oldest grandson graduate. Although they typically stayed with my grandparents when they visited, this time they stayed with us. That night, I was petrified to be in the same room with him. I chose, instead, to sleep on a blow up mattress on the floor of my office. I awoke to find him towering over me – angry and questioning why I was not in his bed where "I belonged". I was afraid. I begged him to leave me alone, to go back to bed, to talk in the morning. But he would not. Instead, he said if I was sleeping there, so was he, and he lay across me on the floor, his full weight pinning me down, refusing to let me escape from underneath him. I still remember the panic, trying to free myself, trying to get away. I finally broke free and ran down the stairs. By that time, the commotion had woken two of my children. My daughter, then just 15 years old, woke her grandparents and said, 'please, help'. What followed was an entire night of rage, all over the house, both inside and out. Mind-numbing rage and ranting that culminated with him saying that he was going to kill me and kill himself and then everyone would be happy. I've been asked before why we did not call the police that night. The only answers I have are that I had tried that in the past and the only result of that reaching out was being told if I did not feel safe to pack my bags and leave, and quite honestly, while all of it was going on, I don't think any of us could think beyond surviving each moment. Thankfully, somehow, we did.

The next day, my father took me to the courthouse and I filed for an order of protection.

I was afraid – afraid they'd say no, afraid he'd come back, afraid I was truly never going to find a way out. But they said yes and I had just the smallest glimmer of hope. I had witnesses, the judge believed me, he wouldn't be able deny who he was anymore...we could break free. He violated that order of protection not long after and we ended up in an Integrated Domestic Violence Court. I was afraid every moment of every day. I was afraid every endless night until I would finally fall asleep from sheer exhaustion only to be woken by a violent nightmare, convinced in my head that he was still there, waiting.

The days and months after, alone with my babies, just trying to survive can only be described as living in a fog of fear and survival, going through the motions of each day without really knowing how we would make it or what was coming next. But we were free, and slowly we started to live a little more each day, breathe a little deeper, smile a little brighter. We were beautifully, amazingly, unbelievably free, and the fog began to lift.

I remember that feeling, that moment in time, when I had the self-realization that I really was going to be alright. I didn't 'need' someone to complete me. I didn't have to define myself by who wanted to be by my side. I had made it through all of this. I was happy, I had incredible kids I loved more than life, family and friends that had stood by me through the darkest of days. I did not know if I was ever going to truly feel 'safe' again, but I knew that I was going to be okay, even if I was alone the rest of my life. I've heard it said that 'love finds you when you stop looking for it'. And that truly was the case for me. A random sequence of events, each one related in a small way to the other, brought me to my best friend. A local band a friend always wanted me to see, but I could never make it before that day, a warm summer's eve, an outdoor show, somehow ending up next to someone my friend had gone to school with and her husband, the daughter of one of their best friends who happened to work at the bar. Suddenly, in the middle of all of these unrelated circumstances, our worlds collided.

I've never believed in love at first sight, and quite honestly, I'm not sure I do today.

What I do believe, however, is that your heart knows. And that night, when Mike and I first met, I truly believe that our hearts knew what we did not. Our hearts knew that there is such a thing as a 'soul mate', a 'love of a lifetime', a 'forever my best friend'. If you are lucky or maybe if you just pay attention, you listen to those faint stirrings of your heart – and you allow everything that can be to become a reality. Looking back it is hard to pinpoint those specific times in our relationship when our feelings moved to the next level – the first 'I only want to be with you', the first 'I love you', or the first 'this is forever'. Looking back it feels as if it always just 'was'. We took things slowly, learning about each other, learning about our lives, our families and our friends. Both of us had been through plenty of 'living'; both good experiences and bad. We knew what mistakes we had each made along the way and we knew what we wanted in a relationship – trust, honesty, commitment, and a friendship that would stand the test of time.

I remember, as a mom, watching my two youngest children, who had been so deeply scarred by the past, form a lasting bond with this man who could have chosen just me, but chose THEM too. I remember feeling the love in my heart growing for him as I watched him become a role model and a father figure to my children who had always deserved that in their lives. I watched as our families became closer, as our kids married, our grandchildren were born, and our bond became stronger.

I have been blessed with the love and support of a man who understands that my past, although it has influenced who I am, does not define me. Mike has stood by me through the tears and the nightmares when they've returned, through the flashbacks and the panic attacks that I will likely always have, and through the times where he paid the price for what another man had done to my psyche. In every one of those moments, I have never doubted his love for me, and I have never doubted his commitment to our relationship, to our life, and to our incredible blended family.

Because of him, I have learned to trust again, to believe again, and to learn how incredible a loving, supportive relationship can be. For that, I will be forever grateful.

On September 3, 2015, Mike and I celebrated our 4th Anniversary. Beautiful flowers, a card and a romantic dinner for two at one of our favorite restaurants. We enjoyed every moment together. After dinner, he excused himself for a minute. I sat there, thinking about how happy I was, how far I had come, how grateful I was for our life together. When Mike walked back to the table, he got down on one knee, and as tears started to roll down my face, he asked me to be his wife. To say I was taken by surprise would be an understatement and I sat there in shock, unable to say a word, long enough that I'm pretty sure he wondered what my answer was actually going to be. It was, of course, yes. One of the hardest things I had to do that weekend was not shout it from the rooftops for all to hear, but our children deserved to hear the news from us first. One by one we talked to all six of them, and received their unanimous approval and support of this next chapter in our lives. That day was four and a half years ago along with three kids getting married, one enlisting and then deploying, and the birth of our three incredible grandchildren. We are often asked by both family and friends, "Are you guys ever actually going to get married?" We always look at each other and laugh at the question. We will indeed, if life ever slows down for two minutes, commit our lives to each other as husband and wife. For now, we are simply happy to take in each moment as our families grow and we attend weddings, baby showers, births and family milestones, knowing that we will forever love each other, forever be best friends, and forever walk through this amazing life we have found together.

What we have together is not perfect because we are not perfect. What we have together is a love for each other that is bigger than both of our imperfections. We have a love and a life that is worth being committed to working through the 'little things' – together – as partners. There was a time when I truly did not believe that I would ever have a relationship like I had seen other people somehow find. There was a time when

I didn't think I even deserved that and I wondered if I was simply too damaged, too broken and too afraid to ever trust my heart again. When I healed enough from my past, when I truly began to love myself again, and when I really believed that I was enough, just as I am, that was when my true light was able to shine.

There is healing in sharing my story and there is also incredible fear. But I made a promise to myself many years ago to no longer let fear control who I am or the choices I make. I am not my past; I am not my mistakes or my scars. My past does not define me, it simply is where I have been. Where ever you are in your journey, whether domestic violence has touched your life in any way or it has not, may the words that help me heal as I put them down on paper for anyone to see give you hope, or inspiration, or simply an understanding of the paths some of us take that most cannot comprehend. We don't wear it on our sleeves for all the world to see. We quietly heal, one step at a time, until the voice inside us is willing to be quiet no more. And when that happens, we rise up from the ashes to be a resounding voice, not just for ourselves, but for all of those who have not yet been able to find their own.

Shanda Roberts

facebook,com/pain2purpose76

twitter.com/pain2purpose76

instagram.com/pain2purpose76

www.pain2purpose76.org

sroberts@pain2purpose76.org

Shanda Roberts was born in Freeport, Bahamas where she lived with her mother who was born in Jamaica & a father who was born in the Bahamas. At the age of 3, her mother moved her & her 3 brothers to Miami for a better life. Later on a 4th brother would be born.

Shanda is a survivor and an advocate of domestic violence. She decided that she wanted to be a support for victims/survivors of this terrible epidemic. She started with collecting new & gently used purses & stuffing them with hygiene products in order to take them to various dv shelters in Miami Dade & Broward counties. This initiative is called the "STUFF-A-PURSE" give-away and the donations came from simply posting what was needed via social media.

She founded Pain 2 Purpose. P2P has given away at least 500 purses to victims living in DV shelters. P2P has a team of 6 which includes her very supportive husband. Shanda is very passionate about supporting victims because she didn't have support when she left her abuser. Forming this organization has helped her in her healing process.

Since her abuse started at a young age, she regularly speaks to teens about how to recognize when they are in an abusive relationship whether physical or emotional. P2P holds a yearly Teen Summit to educate teens and parents about the dangers of teen dating violence, suicide, depression, bullying self-esteem. The organization also hold an "I Am Victorious Survivor's Ball to encourage survivors of abuse and a #Exitplan workshop to give victims resources and strategy plans on how to leave an abusive relationship.

When she's not taking care of her husband, 2 kids at home & one in college she's out speaking in conferences sharing her story. Shanda works in a shelter with teens who are either runaways, truants, ungovernable and/ or locked out. She has won numerous awards from different organizations as well as from radio stations for the work she does in the community. She was named a Beat Blazer by 103.5 The Beat. In May 2020, Shanda was nominated and received her Honorary Doctorate Degree in Ministry from the Trinity Theological Seminary of South Florida. Shanda also has been blessed with the gift of singing. She used to lead praise & worship but now she's taken a step back to see where else God wants to use her. Her gift has blessed her to be able to still reach many. She has sung the National Anthem at a Miami heat game as well as being named the official National Anthem singer for a local bike race in her area.

"I Would've Left ME"

Shanda Roberts

I became what I left. I was violent, aggressive, defensive, and just plain mean. All the while not realizing that I was hurt, broken and confused all while suffering from PTSD. No one could say anything to me that I felt was "disrespectful". No one and nothing was exempt from my pain. Jobs, friendships and relationships, everything was in danger.

I had to learn to love and trust again. It was not easy. I couldn't stay in a stable relationship, friendship or job. No one was exempt from feeling the wrath of my pain. I left jobs just because someone was speaking to me in what I felt was the wrong way. I had friendships that ended because I was always on the defensive and you just weren't gonna handle me any kind of way.

Then I met him…Mr. McDreamy as I love to call him. Well wait, that's not exactly true. Even Mr. McDreamy fell victim to my pain. My life before him was full of turmoil and anger. I was abused sexually, physically, mentally, emotionally and financially. I met my abuser at 15. I married him at 19 and left him for good at 23. Our divorce was finalized in 2000. Not too long after getting divorced, I met the love of my life, George Roberts Jr. a.k.a Mr. McDreamy. We have been together 19 years and married for 18. Mr. McDreamy and I met around October-December of 2000. I'm not exactly sure which month. We both used to ride the bus & the train to get to work. I worked downtown in a small business library and he was working at a hotel on South Beach as a cook. Usually, when you're commuting by public transportation for work you will see the same people everyday. Therefore, I had my eyes on him for a minute. I had a couple of friends who rode the bus and train as well and we would always sit in the back of the bus talking about our day or just laughing and having friendly conversation. There were other riders who would join in on the conversations so the back of the bus used to be a funny venting session on our ride home. George would be in the mix but he sat silently, in his chef's jacket with his headphones on. He wasn't really talkative which instantly got my attention. Later on, he would start conversing with us and then he started bringing little miniature bottles of Remy and he would pass them out to the "back of the bus crew" I was watching him because he looked so good in that chef jacket & those chef pants. I've never seen anyone look so sexy in chef clothes. He likes to joke about this but yeah, I was sweating him and I am not ashamed about it. Well during one of those times when he was passing out the mini's I asked for one which he kindly obliged. That's when the flirting started. I told one of my friends that I was going to have him, and I did. A few days later we would sit away from the group and just talk and get to know each other. That led to a couple of dates and we haven't separated since. He came into the relationship with 3 kids, I had 1 and then we have 2 together. We moved in together shortly after dating and I became pregnant immediately after that. When you 1st start dating, you're usually in a love daze. Living on a cloud with a rainbow and that's where we were, so things moved along rather quickly.

We married 1 year after moving in together. We moved fast but we have learned a lot and we have definitely grown together. When we met, I was not in a position mentally or emotionally to start a new relationship. I was damaged and had not received any help recovering from abuse whatsoever. I thought that since I was not physically in the relationship that I must have been ok. I was sadly mistaken. I was just like the song "Bag Lady" by Erykah Badu. When she sings, "One day all them bags gon' get in your way" and my bags did just that. I carried around a duffle bag full of hurt & pain. I had to learn the hard way that just because you leave a relationship physically does not mean you leave it emotionally. I was a prisoner in my own head. I shared with my husband some of the abuse that I endured and how tumultuous the previous relationship was shortly after we met. I've seen the hurt in his eyes and how he cringes when I talk about the abuse. When someone loves you, they feel your pain. I didn't realize that I was holding on to so much. Our 1st year together was the hardest. Our simple arguments would turn into me screaming and yelling. My aggression was out of control coupled with me being emotional & hormonal due to being pregnant.

Now, let's go back for a minute. My husband has his own story, just to give you an idea of what we both were dealing with. He had his own trust issues with people in general due to how he had to practically raised himself. He had been shot 4 times on 2 separate occasions and didn't have the best relationships either so this was hard for both of us in the beginning. We loved each other but did we trust each other. Now even though we had that rough 1st year, we managed to work through it but we were not out of the woods yet. My husband is very protective because he finally had his own little family, he didn't want anyone to hurt us. However, in my eyes coming from an abusive relationship, that protection looked like "control". He would call me everyday when he got to work and when he was on the way home. I did not do that in the beginning because I didn't feel like I needed to "check-in". One day he told me why that was so important to him and he said "anything can happen from one place to the other and I am just making sure you knew that I was ok and I want to do the same for you". My paranoia from having to really check-in in the last relationship didn't allow me to see that he was generally concerned for me.

Even though we were living life and in love, my aggression slowly got worse. It actually turned into rage because I was determined to not become a victim again. Arguments and disagreements felt like attacks to me. Instead of me realizing that it's ok to have an argument, I went into full defensive mode. The incident that made me realize that I was badly damaged was when George and I got into a disagreement about something. One night, I went out with my friends and he went out by himself. I got upset that he had the nerve to go hang out even though I was out. I know, I know. I had to laugh at myself too. So we got home at the same time and I was telling him to pack his bags and get out. Now, the reason I lashed out at him for going out is because I was the one that had to stay home while my abuser stayed out until all hours of the morning. Now, I felt like I needed to be in control. How dare he go and hangout? Oh no! I was upset! Immediately, I accused him of cheating on me. Of course we're now arguing and he's telling me I need to calm down. Calm down? I didn't even know how to do that at that time. I was now in defense mode because he's yelling. I went to the kitchen and grabbed a knife and while wielding this knife I backed him in a corner. While he's in the corner, I'm daring him to hit me because I just knew that he would, so I'm ready. I was out of my mind and out of control. He threw his hand up to keep me from getting close to him and I came down with that knife and unintentionally cut him on his fingers. Remember I said his profession is to cook so I did more than hurt him physically and draw blood. I don't know what happened but I immediately snapped out of the rage and started crying. When I saw how I hurt the man that I loved and who loved me, I felt horrible. He went to call for an ambulance and I just knew I was going to jail. I was devastated and trying to help him wrap his hand but he didn't even want me to touch him. All I could think was, "what have I done"? I was embarrassed and afraid. I had to sit with him at the hospital and look at what I had done to him. It was that night that I knew I needed help. Our relationship went through some hills and valleys but I thank God that my husband saw through the hurt and pain and decided to stay in our marriage. It took alot of prayer, hard work, love and trust to make it this far. I don't recommend that anyone that has suffered abuse to go and start a relationship until they have seeked counseling. I suffer from PTSD and I didn't know it at that time. I took all of my anger out on the one person who was trying to love me like I am supposed to be loved. When you're used to being mistreated you don't know how to accept gifts or even kind words. To a survivor, they feel like something may follow that action. I used to be in fear every day, so quick movements would make me flinch. I learned that me lashing out at my husband was because I was trying to sabotage my relationship in fear that I would be hurt again. Being in a healthy loving relationship was something that I thought I would never experience. That was the furthest thing in my mind when I met him but it has been one of my biggest blessings. I have truly learned how to love, receive love and I have learned to trust again. I had to learn that everyone is not out to hurt me. It didn't seem reachable but I can tell you that it is wonderful. I love Mr. McDreamy with everything in me. He has been my support system in everything I have had to endure since we have gotten together. When I had to have surgery and was in the hospital for 21 days, his face was the first face I saw when I woke up. I can't go to any singing event or speaking event without him praying for me. He is my rock! Love after abuse didn't seem possible for me but it also would not have been attainable if I didn't 1st learn how to love myself. Although Mr. McDreamy makes me happy, it's not his responsibility to do so. I had to learn that that came from me. Self love was my responsibility and it's yours too. I am able to love him so much better because I love me first.

Hadassah Shalon

Nikki Bryan a.k.a. *The Soul Maiden* was raised in Brooklyn, NY until her family relocated to the state of Florida in 1988. After graduating from high school, she decided to enter the school of hard knocks. After learning many hard-fought lessons, she married and raised two amazing children. Ms. Bryan earned her bachelor's degree from Belhaven University and then as a single parent continued to earn her master's degree in Mental Health Counseling from Palm Beach Atlantic University. She currently serves as the Vice President on the Board of Directors for the Beautifully Unblemished Vitiligo support group. Ms. Bryan's personal mission is to share her experiences, failures, and triumphs in order to uplift and emotionally support others. She embraces the credo "Love of Self Versus Love of Others, No One Should be Forced to Choose". Ms. Bryan believes that there is a need for broader conversations in order to continually remind everyone of the emotional, physical, and negative social impacts of surviving trauma.

Roulette

Hadassah Shalom

Love of Self Versus Love of Others; No One Should be Forced to Choose

When you find yourself staring down the barrel of a gun, your thoughts start coming at you real fast. Inevitably one of them will be how did I end up here? It was not one big moment for me, it was lots of little moments. Where were the signs when we first met? Why did I not realize that this man was a psychopath? What is my family going to say? What if a bullet comes flying out of that chamber? My mind, ever so ready to console me…you will not know, you will already be dead. Well I guess that was some small consolation, but you know what? I wasn't ready to die.

The streets were hot, all the time. Every day was a hustle and a struggle all at once. I was young and constantly on the hunt for everything bad to get into. I loved going to the reggae club with my friends, blowing trees, driving crazy, and men; but most of all I loved a challenge. If I saw something and I wanted it, I would just take it, but it is true what the elders say, "be careful what you ask for". This was a trait that proved to be dangerous and put me in enough bad situations to last a lifetime, one of those situations was Rashad.

There are things that we tell ourselves to quiet all the voices and hide the red flags; but when you are a strong headed person you just want what you want; the first time I saw Rashad I decided he was going to be mine.

I used to see him at the club, wavy hair, brown skin, and a beautiful gold smile. The smile is what got you; it lit up his face and lit up the room. I already knew he was Jamaican; muscle thick, he was a little shorter than me but that was a small thing; no pun intended. What he lacked in stature he made up for in clout and big chains. He always had an audience; he was popular because he was a top boy, a dealer. I was nineteen and he was enough to capture my imagination. I had always been confident about myself when it came to the hunt, so I set out to do what it took.

We all know the formula; conveniently be in his line of sight a couple times, catch him looking, meet his gaze; and hit him with the smile…gold grills dazzling. We ended up dancing a couple of times, a little slow whine to show I meant business and we struck up a conversation. He was a few years older than me, Caribbean and from New York. Oh, we have so much in common. Our backgrounds gave us plenty to talk about and we ended the night on a nice note. I hoped I would see him again soon.

A couple of months go by and I didn't see Rashad around; but one night I spot him! Guess who's back...hmmm I wonder where he's been...at some point I made my way over to where he was standing just like I was supposed to. We made plans to meet at the Caribbean restaurant upstairs later that night. I make my way there and he was already at a table, I sat down and we resumed our conversation. Talking to him was easy. I asked him, "So where you been the past couple of months?" He said, "In jail without the bail." I brushed the information off. He ordered steamed red snapper, oh he got money. I didn't want to overplay my hand, so I just ordered something cheap. He told me he was staying at the hotel, I called him Ra, he called me Red Snapper. It was the early 90s, I was feeling so exclusive.

We spent the night together. I told him I could not stay all night because I lived with my mom still, he understood. He was adequate, but he was kind, and I enjoyed being around him. He looked at me somewhere around 3am and said, "There's forty dollars in the top drawer so you can take a cab home." Yes, even back then it was forty dollars. Well at least he knows how to treat a lady, I really liked him, but I did not expect to hear back from him. I was sure we would run into each other on his corner or at the club, but I came, I saw, I conquered. I was good. He beeped me the next day. I smiled to myself...I guess we go together now.

At first everything was a breeze, there was status attached to being with Ra. Whenever I hit the corner, I got respect, at the club I got respect, from the females I got hate but I was a conceited person back then, I did not care. They were supposed to hate, that was their job. I was so conceited that I brazenly told my mother that I was dating a drug dealer. Like that would give me status with my mom. After telling her about him the next words out of my mouth were "Ra...my mom put me out". He told me not to worry, I packed a bag and headed downtown to meet up with him at his "job". He peeled two hundred dollars off a stack and told me to go rent a room. I felt so grown, like I had a man that would take care of me and treat me like a woman. Pipe dreams.

Rashad was a charmer, and when he smiled, he had twinkles in his eyes that would bedazzle. I will never forget the first day I saw that smile freeze and those eyes turn to black coal. There was an album out at the time, Ice Cube Predator; I let that cassette play back to back and rapped all the lyrics. One night Rashad came home, swinging a half empty bottle of Hennessey in his hand as usual; he sat on the bed. "Red," he slurred looking up at me, his eyes were glazed and watery. "Yes" I answered. "Why you always playing that g-dd-m tape! I'm sick of hearing that sh-t!" I was so naïve I didn't think anything of what he was asking me. I just replied, "What's the problem? It's my music I like it." The last thing I remembered was seeing the Hennessey bottle swing up in the air and several hours later I woke up on the floor.

My head was throbbing, it took me a few minutes to piece together what had happened. Did he hit me? It seemed incomprehensible; Rashad had never shown any indication that he could be that person. I pulled myself off the floor and walked to the mirror, my face was intact, but I felt a knot on my scalp. I pulled my hand away, no blood. Good. I walked to the door and stepped out onto the second story balcony. Our room overlooked the pool. There was Rashad, fully clothed in the pool drunkenly splashing around in the water and pulling all the tape out of the cassette, the empty bottle of Hennessey laying on the concrete.

Ra looked up, saw me standing there and yelled out, "You wanna listen to somebody every day you gonna listen to me. You see what you made me do? I cant swim, I'm gonna just let myself drown in here" He let himself sink below the surface and abandoning all regard for my own wellbeing I ran down the stairs and begged him to get out of the pool. I pleaded with him not to hurt himself and told him that I loved him. He climbed out and passed out on the concrete right next to his empty bottle. Why didn't I realize in that moment that the logic had already become twisted?

Every day my fear of Rashad grew like an insidious little seed planted in the core of my soul. It was watered and fertilized by his drunken episodes. He would come home from work full of self-loathing, lashing out at me for even the smallest indiscretions. If I didn't have the food he was in the mood for or didn't do the laundry correctly or iron his clothes properly it would set him off. His favorite game? Russian Roulette. He would take his gun, spin the barrel, put it right up to my chest and pull the trigger. Click. I started secretly drinking in order to cope with the terror, I hid the bottles under the bed so he couldn't find them.

There was one night he met me at the front of the hotel and demanded to know what I had bought for dinner. I worked at a seafood restaurant at the time and I told him I bought him some fish and fries. He grabbed the bag from me and opened it, "It's cold" he glared at me. My heart started to race red alert, placate! red alert, placate! "Baby," I responded with a weak smile, "You know I take the bus home; I'll heat it up for you." He balled the bag up, "Get your ass to the room, and if I make it there before you, I'm going to beat the hell out of you." I took off like a shot oh my God I cannot let him hit me again! I made it back to the room before him. He didn't beat me. I fell asleep with one eye open thinking to myself, well at least he plays fair.

One day Ra told me that it was okay if my best friend Sharise came to visit. I had not seen her or anyone in my family for that matter in the three months since I moved in with him. Her and I spent the day together catching up, blowing trees and walking the strip. We were so close and shared everything including each other's secrets. We even looked alike, people always thought we were sisters. But even though I told her that Rashad was strict, I could not bring myself to tell her about the physical abuse. I was embarrassed and did not want her to know how I was living. Besides, since I been with him, he had only hit me a couple of times. It wasn't that bad.

Ra came home, less drunk than usual. I introduced him to Sharise and told him she was getting ready to call a cab to go home. He nodded at her and turned to me, 'Red, come outside let me talk to you for a minute." I turned to Sharise as we headed out the door and mouthed to her that I would be right back. We step out onto the balcony, I tried to keep my voice steady, "What's up baby?" He looked at me with those coal eyes, "Tell your friend she's not leaving" I didn't think I heard him correctly, so I said, "Come again?" He repeated what he said. I asked him what he was talking about. He responded "she looks just like you, there's two of you?. I want both of y'all, she's staying with us. I'm going back down to the spot. Take her home to get her stuff and come back" He turned and walked off, I was not going to argue with him. He turned and looked back at me, eyes dark as a storm, "And don't think about not coming back. If you ever try to leave me, I will find you, and I will kill you." I watched him walk away in slow motion. Dazed, I stepped back into the room.

Sharise asked me what happened, I told her. I told her all that had been going on between Rashad and I as well as what he said to me outside. I looked her in the eye and told her "He said you gotta come back, if you don't I don't know what he's gonna do." At first Sharise looked shocked, but then an air of resignation came over her. She said, "Well if he say I gotta come back then that's what I better do" It didn't occur to me at the time that she did not put up a whole lot of resistance to the idea. I was too busy giving in to the utter dread of what would happen to me if she didn't come back. And a small part of me was relieved that there would be someone there to take the pressure off me when Ra would get into his moods.

Sharise moved in. I suffered all the indignities that come with sharing a partner under the threat of physical harm. I swallowed my pride to protect my body. If Ra thought I had even the slightest attitude towards the living arrangement there was hell to pay. He claimed that since he treated us equally and paid for everything that there was nothing for me to be upset about. Sharise became ill and I had to go to the store and get her some medicine. Ra got it into his head that I took too long because I was hating on Sharise and wanted her to suffer. When I got home, he hit me so hard upside my head that I needed the medicine more than Sharise did.

The next day I began to take stock of my situation. There was no way this way of life could continue. My family would be appalled if they knew the ordeal I was going through. The fear of Ra was very real but then I had a thought, if my father and brothers knew what was happening, they would kill this man. This idea gained traction in my mind because I loved the men in my family way too much to expose them to a situation like this. The nurturing that I received as a daughter and a sister helped me to realize that I did not have to accept the treatment that I was enduring. In a twisted way I also thought I love Ra too much to stay with him. I had to leave him for his own sake because my menfolk did not need to be involved in a war with a drug dealer.

When Ra left for work, I asked Sharise if she wanted to leave, I was terrified to ask her because if she told Ra I really feared that he would follow through on his threats to kill. I did not know who her loyalty was to at this point, but if she wanted out, I would not leave her behind. She looked at me and said yes, I took her at her word, and we started to plan.

Since we didn't have to pay any bills, we saved our paychecks for two weeks, hiding them under the mattresses. The day of our escape arrived, when we were sure that Ra had gotten in a taxi, we grabbed the checks and ran down to street to the check cashing place. We went to 7-11 to grab some food, came back to the hotel, and rented a room the next floor up.

We moved all our stuff into the new room, since we had no car this was the quickest way to get all our stuff moved out before Ra came back.

We hid out in the room with the lights off, eating 7-11 and scared as hell for two days. I peeked through the curtains and scoped the parking lot, the coast looked clear. We called a cab, one of the van ones; we loaded everything in it and told the driver to haul tail. As I watched the hotel grow smaller and smaller in my rear view, I felt melancholy and hollow. I felt like it might not be the end of the story. In my heart I was deathly afraid that Ra might find me one day, but I also knew that on that day, in that moment; the love that I had for myself was greater than the fear. On that day, I bet on me.

Karen Martin Bobbitt

As someone who experienced all aspects (emotional, verbal, and physical) of Domestic Violence during her 20 year first marriage, Karen can say unequivocally getting out is easier said than done but so very worth it. Her divorce went on far too long due to her ex-husband's tactics to continue to control all facets of her life through continued threats of violence, allegations to law enforcement of bank and mail fraud, and demands for personal and real property. Completing her Associate's Degree in Paralegal studies with Honors during the course of her separation and divorce, she stood firm in her resolve to leave the life of Domestic Violence behind her and made it through even the darkest of days towards a very bright future.

Karen has been a successful businesswoman, having worked in the Purchasing field for over 20 years. Her resume includes several Fortune 100 companies along with family owned businesses. Taking time to heal, physically and emotionally, Karen focused on establishing her own network of friends and learning to enjoy the peace and quiet of a life without constant shame and pain.

Nearly seven years from the last time her ex-husband laid hands on her, she met someone who would change her entire attitude about trusting men and marriage. Karen and her new husband, Steve, have been building a loving and caring life together and look forward to decades of love, respect, and happiness together.

Amaryllis

Karen Martin Bobbitt

The Amaryllis is an amazing plant. Its native habitat tends to repress its growth, and thereby prevent it from blooming. In mountainous and rocky areas overshadowed by the dense overgrowth of other plants its beauty waits. Not until after the heat and flames of brush fires strip the ground bare will these plants receive the sun needed to bloom and become everything it was always meant to be. Strong, beautiful, and above all, resilient. It took a very long time before the smoldering coals of my own personal hell exploded into a massive inferno, clearing the way, giving me the air, and the light to reach for a life I had come to believe would never been experienced, except in dreams. It was during that inferno I took control. The fire no longer threatened to consume me, rather it began to fuel me. I discovered how strong, beautiful, and truly resilient I could be.

I was young and rather naïve when I married my abuser. Of course, back then he was not abusive. Hindsight being 20/20 and all that jazz, the signs were there. They always are. He was the drummer in a local house band, long hair, snakeskin boots. Rocking the late 80's 'hair metal' thing. Let us just say that this was not my typical crowd. I had graduated high school shortly before meeting him and was one of those students who enjoyed learning and challenged myself with Advance Placement classes where possible. He was a long-haired high school dropout drummer in a going nowhere rock and roll band. My parents were not impressed.

Growing up, my family was what I believed typical. My parents were not divorced, and were, in fact, happily married. Rarely did my younger sister and I observe even raised voices between them. I cannot remember being spanked by either of them. My homelife was a peaceful and happy one. I mention this because we see and hear so often of the statistics for folks to end up in abusive relationships because they grew up as a child of one. My case is not one of those. My father died in October 2011, and that is when the abuse intensified, drastically so.

In the beginning my abuser paid attention to me. And for someone who had one boyfriend during high school, which began and ended during my sophomore year, I was not accustomed to being on the receiving end of romantic attention. And so, we dated. When I say dated, I mean that I paid for everything, drove us everywhere, and frankly was the one who put in the effort of being in the relationship. When you notice that you are the only one in the relationship making all the efforts and sacrifice, stop. That is not a loving relationship, and it will become servitude from which it is difficult to escape.

We met in early Fall 1989, married December 1990. I was nineteen years old. His temper scared me, but it had not been directed at me yet, so I was not too concerned. Small things happened at first. He would get mad when I got a haircut. Seriously mad and would pout for days. He would complain that we did not do things together because I continued having Saturday morning outings with my mom and sister. So, I stopped going with them. I did not have many friends, which meant being preoccupied with gal-pal activities was not a problem. Isolation is the key to control in abusive relationships. I was isolated early in mine.

My first experience with physical abuse occurred 11 years into the marriage in 2001, a day or two before my birthday. He slapped me across the face after throwing and breaking plates in a fit of anger. I was stunned. This was the moment I never thought would happen, and if it did, I knew exactly what I was going to do. However, thoughts and actions are two very different things. My abuser spent the next week being apologetic, kind and loving. I stayed and never said a word to anyone. Appearances matter donchaknow?

It was a long while before he physically attacked me again. In the interim, the negative comments and isolation continued. The only friends I had were his friends. My hobbies were ones he thought I should do. I attended nursing school because that was what he wanted. I even began to collect things because he thought I should. I had a few salt and pepper shaker sets which held sentimental value for me. Suddenly I had 50 or more sets. Same thing with depression era glass. Oh, and again with sugar and creamer sets. Stuff, things, baubles, and trinkets were what should make me proud and happy, according to my abuser. They did not.

I never dressed right, or wore the right makeup, or perfume, or shoes. My hair was never right. "Why don't you wear any of the jewelry I spent money on for you?" "Why can't you take some pride in how you look?" "Why can't you keep up with cleaning this house? Or mowing the yard?" Or a million other things I could not do right. He worked away from home for most of our marriage, so expecting to have things just right when he was home from out of town should not have been so hard. Right? No matter what, I could not do anything correctly or to his expectations.

Some of the physical abuse I suffered included: being beaten while I sat in the passenger seat of a vehicle he was driving while on a highway going over 55; being forced out of the car, and left standing on the side of the road until he decided to turn around to pick me up; having a food processor thrown across the kitchen at me, narrowly missing my head (to this day I still have that food processor – yes it works - although I am sure Cuisinart does not recommend their appliances be handled so rough!); riding as a passenger in the car while he floored the accelerator threatening to drive us into the side of the mountain while slapping me; and nearly dislocating my hip in order to have sex because I was not responding enthusiastically enough.

All the verbal, mental, and physical abuse I had experienced in my 21-year marriage paled in comparison to the night when everything changed. You see, in early 2012 we had agreed to divorce. Oh, I failed to mention that he had at least two affairs during the last few years of our marriage, and he was actively engaged in one of that had been going on for at least six months at the time of separation. I do not know if there were others, but I would not be surprised if there had been. Not only did I forgive abuse over and over, I forgave adultery more than once. Because, as he informed me multiple times, it was my fault that he cheated.

My abuser was not happy with how we were dividing up things. He demanded money to leave the home, lots of money that I would have to get from my mother. I said no. He snapped. I found myself being attacked with a kitchen chair, yanked from my chair by my hair and slammed face first onto the kitchen floor to be hit, kicked, and stomped repeatedly. When he left the room, for a split second, I believed the assault was over, until I heard the slide of the 12-gauge Winchester racking in shells. Before I heard the footsteps of him making his way back to the kitchen, I grabbed my keys and ran.

My abuser never saw the inside of a jail cell. Apparently, he was never even handcuffed. He violated protective orders repeatedly. Mailed me letters begging to come home, or at least to meet him somewhere to talk. My favorite was the one he sent the week of my birthday a few months after the attack, remind me "that I have never missed your birthday before, I don't want to start now" mixed in with threats of all kinds. From then on, I handed the letters to my attorney, unopened. He challenged every protective order renewal. My abuser filed complaints against me with the local Postmaster for tampering with the mail (I was writing no longer at this address and return to sender on them before handing them back to the postal carrier). He went to the police in the city adjacent where we lived to accuse me of bank fraud. Neither of these went anywhere, other than a courtesy contact by each to let me know they had ended up investigating him because of his accusations once they noted the charges against him along with the protective orders. Friends of my abuser contacted me to accuse me of lying, to threaten me. I changed my phone number multiple times, giving it out only when necessary. My abuser was employing every intimidation tactic he could to get me to break and talk to him.

Court ordered anger management made my abuser worse. The bailiffs even made mention of the change in him and his story as time went on. He has begun to twist things around to make him the victim of what was inflicted upon me. At the conclusion of his probation, he was free and clear. Allowed to legally own and carry guns. I was required to hand over to him guns we had owned during the marriage. To this day, I have the Winchester 12 gauge that I fully believe he intended to use to end my life on February 5, 2012.

No one in my life knew any of what I had been through. I had one new friend who was not his, all the of my other acquaintances were his friends first and foremost. My family had no idea that they were seeing only what I allowed them to see. I had not walked on eggshells in my home, instead I navigated my way through a minefield every single day. Eggshells only make noise under your feet. Mines, well mines will injure, maim, and kill you.

Getting out of that minefield took some doing, the system is not perfect by any stretch. I had to partially disrobe in front of two male deputies in a teleconference with the substitute magistrate to receive my-Emergency Order of Protection. My attorney asked me pointed questions about seeing this through, or was I going to reconcile with my abuser. The Commonwealth Attorney had me come in for a very similar discussion before proceeding with prosecution.

The minefield had blown up and the was damage significant, but I survived and began to find my way out of a darkness which had consumed me for so very long. Slowly I told my mom things I had never wanted her to know. I reconnected with a friend from high school. Along with the girlfriend I had made in my classes as the local community college, I now had three people to support me. Then came another, and another, then lo and behold yet another! Contrary to what I had come to believe, I was not so terrible after all. In the words of one of the best SNL characters ever, Stuart Smalley, *"I'm Good Enough, I'm Smart Enough, and Doggone It, People Like Me! "*

My abuser went through three attorneys during our divorce, which took far longer than reasonable for a couple with no children thanks to his never-ending demands. The first one "fired" him after the first hearing, realizing his client had lied to him. The second apologized to me in open court for what my abuser had done to me. She retired and moved out of town within two weeks of the signing of the divorce decree. The third, was left dealing with an angry client who demanded the divorce be appealed and reheard for reasons which were literally incomprehensible. Which of course did not happen.

Over the next few years, I leaned on my mother and my friends heavily. I declared all the time, "I am NEVER getting married again!". They laughed, and I protested. Even dated a couple of times. Headlines of domestic violence murders, and murder-suicides became all I saw on the news, serving to reinforce my alone and safe mindset. Eventually though I met someone and, wanting to see the good, began accepting being second, third and an even more distant number in order of importance to him. He had a good job, had been there for almost 30 years, everybody seemed to love him, and he drank. He drank a lot. The biggest part of this 'relationship' was me getting called in the middle of the night to pick him up from one of his regular places, take him to get food in him and then getting him home safely. He was never violent. But he was not good to me, even though I told myself that he was.

One night, I was of the understanding that I was picking up pizza and heading to his place for an evening on the couch watching TV. Dinner was in my car, and as I pulled up to his place, I noticed a car which looked very much like the one belonging to his former girlfriend. In I walked with the pizza and there they were, snuggled up on the couch watching TV. After introducing myself to her and collecting my belongings, I dropped his key, took back mine and walked out the door. Here is the thing though, it did not hurt. There were no tears. And with no better option before me, he bounced back and forth, off and on, between us for a couple of years. It could have been worse, I had experienced worse. Maybe people just cheated.

Because of the damage inflicted by my abuser that fateful night, knee replacement surgery was going to be necessary. And so, five and a half years after that assault a new knee was meant to be. The man I had been seeing on and off did not come visit me during the three days I was in the hospital. Nor did he come to my house to check on me or visit during the following weeks. Once I was healed up though, he was ready for me to be his designated driver all over again. And evidently, I was ready too, because that is exactly what happened. He was selfish and manipulative, but he needed me. Turns out not so much. The game of hot potato in which I was a willing participant continued, he would pick up right where he left off with me when he got bored of her. And visa versa.

In the middle of year 2018, I was presented a new employment opportunity which I gladly accepted. You see, despite my apparent inability to stand up for myself in my personal life, I was able to be very in control in my professional life. Work as a Purchasing Manager can get uncomfortable. Pricing negotiations can be tense, and conflict is a part of the day to day. Get this, I love it! I have been extremely successful in my professional life because of my bulldoggedness (I know that is not a real word, but it creates an appropriate mental picture, does it not?). Why I take shit in my personal life and not at work is a question I simply cannot answer.

Alright, let us get on with the reason we are gathered here together today. But I get ahead of myself. As I mentioned, middle of 2018, new job. Things are going well, Purchasing is more of less the same anywhere you go, the widgets and whatnots may be different, but the process is the same. I am meeting all my co-workers, getting into the groove of things, making myself at "home" so to speak. One of my co-workers is the Plant Electrician and Maintenance Mechanic, Steve. One of the areas I was looking into making improvements involved equipment he had responsibility to keep up and running. Early on we had a lot of interaction. Not necessarily daily, but a couple of times a week.

Now I can sense the 'uh-ohs' already starting out there. "You don't get your honey, where you make your money", and other cruder sayings with the same meaning. The YOU DO NOT DATE A CO-WORKER has always been a hard and fast rule for me. I have seen the results of dating relationships between co-workers turn sour, and the work environment can become very treacherous. I have always had easier friendships with men than women, and I had no reason to even consider my work relationship with Steve would move beyond a work hours friendship.

Over several months we chatted more frequently about things outside of work. He was in the throes of ending a relationship with a woman he had lived with for several years. Steve seemed to have some of the character traits (flaws) as me. He took care of people and did not give up. If you were to have found either of us on the Titanic, we would have been helping everyone else to lifeboats and using teacups to bail the water back into the ocean. Steve had full custody of his young daughter from a previous marriage. He worked seven days a week to take care of her, his girlfriend, and others. But still he smiled. He was kind and respectful. When Steve asked how you were doing, it was not just a phrase you say in passing, he was interested to know and to help if he could.

Every Friday, Steve and a few others would go out to lunch as a group, and eventually I was asked to join them. By one of the other members of this little lunch crew, not Steve. There was this one Friday when the others were either busy or had taken the day off, and the remaining lunch crew available were Steve and me. We got along fine and always seemed to have things to talk about, so we went on without everybody else. We ended up talking a good bit longer than our lunch hour, but it was great to have someone to talk with who had similar bad experiences with the opposite sex. We understood the hurt the other had gone through, or good at least put ourselves in the other's shoes. I found myself spilling the ugliness of how and why my marriage ended, to explain why I was never ever going to get married again. Steve would tell me more of the unpleasant details of his previous marriage and his current falling apart relationship, then make that same declaration about remaining single from now on. I had found myself a friend and a kindred spirit, keeping in mind that he is a man and eventually he would show himself to be like all the rest.

Over the next couple of months, we would speak more frequently and slowly reveal our nerdy side to one another. He shared pictures of his daughter and talked about things they enjoyed doing together. Steve and I are the same age, and we shared a lot of the same memories of television shows, movies, and music. Finally, someone who would get my goofy movie references and not roll his eyes. Eventually we started to text and talk on the phone outside of work hours. Our friendship was getting stronger and we shared a mutual understanding and respect for the other. Work was work; personal life was personal. This was not something we even had to talk about, which was refreshing.

Several years ago, I had found a meme and posted it on my Facebook page: "I would like to find the male version of me. That would be epic". Found myself starting to realize Steve was that person, and that was indeed epic. We talked about the things we were doing outside of work: things around the house, working on our cars, etc.; and he was not bothered at all by the fact that I did so many things myself. Once when talking with one of my best friends about why I was not dating, he told me that it was kind of my own fault. That I was intimidating to most men and saying something to the effect that a man does not want to have a woman who does not need him. I looked at him and stated simply, "That sounds a lot like the kind of insecure man I have already been around, and if that is how all of you are, that is your problem."

I would show Steve pictures of projects I had going on at my place in the country, my tractor, snapping turtles I had pulled from the pond, and may other things. He never flinched, seeming more and more interested in what I had to say and what I was doing. Steve was well-liked at work. I began to pay close attention when I heard his name come up. Never did I hear anything negative thing. The folks I worked closest with would say mention how great a guy he is, he would do anything for you, and on and on. Still, I was waiting for that Mr. Hyde moment.

We would talk late into the evenings and I found myself laughing more than I had in longer than I could remember. My mom had been living with me for a couple of years at this point and would frequently ask me if I had "laid an egg' upstairs, after one of those long phone conversations. It was a nice change from my usual routine of grumbling, grubbing, and going to bed during the week. Even though I very much liked this new job, I had a commute of an hour each way, so grumbling was pretty much a given every evening during the week. As great as those nighttime phone calls were, I was still waiting for the red flags to start popping up.

I would like to think no one at work knew we were talking, but a number of those close to him knew. A few others had suspicions, but there never seemed to be any rumors going around. That made a big impression on me concerning how much our co-workers thought of him. Steve was unable to attend our company Christmas party because his daughter had a mild fever. We shared our disappointment, but I told him that putting his child first was more important, and I respected him very much for being such an attentive father. Steve mentioned to me later that what I had said meant so much to him and was not at all the reaction he was prepared for. That is when I realized that he was waiting for Ms. Hyde to appear, as much as I was remaining prepared for the inevitable appearance of Mr. Hyde…

One evening, shortly thereafter, when we were in the middle of another long phone conversation we started talking about Christmas, and what the other typically does for the holiday. Steve had talked about his family a few times, so I already had the impression that they were a large and close-knit bunch. We both look back on this conversation and have a good laugh often. You see, Steve starts hemming and hawing about Christmas Eve dinner being at the home of his aunt and uncle every year and how everybody is there. Then he starts up like he is going to ask me something, but giving me a way out with this whole, "I know it would be a long drive for you to come back this way on a day off, but I was wondering if, well maybe……". Me thinking cool, movie or dinner somewhere is where this is leading, and it would be nice to get together outside of work for a change and see how he is in the 'real world', I say, "Just spit it out Steve". And just like that I have been invited to his family's Christmas Eve dinner!

I agreed, because what better way to find out if I should run sooner rather than later, than to meet his family? I should have run after the first holiday dinner with my abuser's family! I have to say that first date with Steve was atypical at best. My friends thought I had lost my mind. Honestly, I thought that I had as well. It was the best thing that could have happened though. Holidays can be stressful, and people tend to be more emotional (good and bad) during family holiday events. Plus, it allowed Steve to get a look at how I was in a setting that had me under the microscope of the people who loved him most. I even gave him a peck on the cheek at the end of the evening. On my drive home this glimmer of hope that we were heading down the 'more than just friends' territory had begun to glow brighter. Still I was waiting.

Steve, his daughter, and I spent New Year's Eve together. We went to see Bumblebee; you know the adorable yellow car from The Transformers movies. Come on people, his daughter had just turned eight. It was a more appropriate choice than The Mule. Besides, he and I are sci-fi nerds, so it was great for us too. I found that I was looking for Mr. Hyde less and less. Not once during our months of texting had I received a single dick pic from him. And ladies, we all know that seems to be the first thing a guy sends after you give him your number. He was never rude, crude, or lewd during our phone calls. He was the epitome of a gentleman all the time.

We began to spend more and more time together; he even met and was immediately loved by my mom. Steve would tell me that he felt a peace with me that he had never experienced before. I even let him work on my car. That is when my all my friends knew this was true love. I never let anybody work on my vehicles. Waiting for the other shoe to drop became looking toward the future with this man and his daughter. He has a very soft heart and feels the pain of others like it were his own. I have seen him tear up, unashamedly, at things which made me tear up. We sensed each other's moods, and distress. My ability to trust a man without reservation had taken shape.

I discovered the second affair of my abuser because he had begun to hide his phone. One day I went looking for it and found it, along with the texts and photos I suspected existed.

When the on-again/off-again fella from the previous few years would become more careful about leaving his phone lying around, I would wait for opportunities to look at it. What I would see reassured me that men could not be trusted. A cell phone certainly makes communicating on the sly easier. I will not say that I did not consider going through Steve's phone, because I did think about it. I even picked it up once intending to do just that. Then I laid it back down. Not one time had he given me a reason not to trust him. To this day I have not gone through his phone, or his wallet. Mr. Hyde was not coming, and I know he never will.

Steve and I began looking at homes, discussing the future, our future, as though it were a given. In each other we had found our absolute best friend, our soulmate. Now this is not to say that I did not adhere to one of the steadfast rules of a domestic violence survivor. I did a background check. I searched his name in the court system public records for the county in which he lived, the surrounding counties and cities where he lived previously. He knows this, and he understood exactly why. If your next partner in a relationship to be reacts in a manner other than understanding, there is your red flag if there has not already been one.

By the standards of many people we know, we moved very fast. Our first date was Christmas Eve and just before St Patrick's Day we were putting a contract on a house, announcing our "It Just Got Real" engagement, and giving people "Save the Date" info for a July wedding. Co-workers at bosses at our job who were not "in the know" were shocked as we began to publicly disclose our relationship. If your workplace is anything like ours, when it comes to the grapevine of information, the fact that it was not common knowledge to every single person is amazing.

We closed on our home the first week of May and married the last week of July. I would say that we spent the next 6 months moving and consolidating households. Steve, his daughter, my mother, and me. One big happy family. Sometime before the wedding my mom looked at me and said that if she died today, she would die happy because she knew I was safe and happy, and not going to be alone anymore.

Almost seven years from the split of my first marriage to the decision to marry again, is what my 'healing period' consisted of. I continue to see a psychiatrist every four months and take medication which helps me manage the anxiety that will likely be with me always. Steve and I are closing in on our first anniversary, and I have not looked for Mr. Hyde in ages. We are truly the best of friends above all else.

I liken my hard-fought love for myself to the growth and bloom of the Amaryllis. The band Shinedown, released their album Amaryllis, shortly after the end of my first marriage.

That album became the soundtrack for what I was going through, and the title track was, especially healing. In an interview, Brent Smith of Shinedown explained that to them the Amaryllis is all about destiny. "It's all about perseverance and about rising above and blooming in front of the world and being an individual and being a visionary and showing the world your true colors. That's what it represents because it's a flower that grows in the desert in a time of year where there's really not a good explanation as to how it grows and how it looks so strong."

Much like the Amaryllis plant, I endured the darkness, suffered the flames, found the sun. I have grown, become strong, and let me you, like that beautiful flower ***I have bloomed.***

Harley Dree

Facebook.com/HarleyDree

ThriveLife.com/HarleyDree

Ms.HarleyDree@gmail.com

Harley Dree is an experienced photographer, adventurer, and creative. Driven by passion for joy and knowledge, she takes pride in providing the best Still Moment to cherish possible. As an independent Digital Travel Photographer, her goals include seeing all God has created, adding warm reminders in picture form to her clients' homes, and showing the world from her own uniquely obscure perspective. Along the way she jumps at any chance to try new things, especially in the culinary realm. She has captured images in over 45 countries with the rest of the globe still on her wanderlust list.

In addition to her primary focus of creating art, Harley has been active in online sales for many years. Currently she is helping educate healthy easy eating with Thrive Life Foods.

Harley has been recognized for her extraordinary commitment to sharing encouragement and going headstrong towards whatever her present goal is. Fear does not seem to be a word she was born with as it shows no signs of holding her back. Harley resides in the southern part of Alabama at this time. She spent her early years on the west coast; in adulthood being nomadic has not felt strange to her. Living in many states, even obtaining German residency. To this day, always eager to pick up and see more, she has cultivated a multitude of connections worldwide.

Growing up as an only child to a single mom, who did not instill the belief of boredom, clearly contributed to Harley finding ways to embrace and enjoy any moment, even the stillness when graced with it. She has been blessed with two matching rescue beagles who have a story all their own and might well be more traveled than you. Her desire to learn and constantly expand is obvious through the classes, courses, events, seminars, and more that find their way on her schedule. The variedness of Harley's resume shows how she is always seeking to keep life exciting while obtaining new skills.

Now in her early 30s, Dree has professed that this is by far her best decade yet, emphasis heavily placed on the word yet. "I have changed from simply promising *things will be interesting* to manifesting a life which promotes *good-interesting*. I am grateful for that newly added criteria." Harley truly appreciates your time given to read these bits of her life's journey thus far.

Relinquishing The Habit Of Hiding

Harley Dree

I am doing it again

Open transparency, without self-shaming, I admit here in line two I have been doing it for weeks. The more I reflect on my first three decades, I have been disturbed by the hard awakening of the frequency I was taught how to do it at so many junctures. I pray you never have to personally understand what it is, but if you do come to a point where you start to follow suit, then my prayer is for you to notice your collusion with it quickly. I am encouraged by my awareness when figuring out it has slipped in once more. I want to open up with you, which leaves no room for me second guessing all I have to say. It can not get in the way. I do not have to put on a show for you or let my hesitancy weasel in. My place right now is to share without shield because the filters and framing are what help perpetuate the horrifying growth of abuse that surrounds likely all of us, closer than we care to admit.

With it out of the way by bringing light to my doubts, I deserve to be here. I more than appreciate you entering into this time alongside me. Though not as alluring as a movie, poetry segment, fairytale, parable, or extremely philosophical insight, I believe there is quite a lot to be grasped from the below short burst of my life. These paragraphs, as all survivor exposés, do have the power to change and even possibly save lives. I am choosing to get over my own concerns for you, those you love, coworkers, neighbors, really anyone you interact with, by no means limited to just your inner circles.

We all only have this one life. It is no one's right or place to bury us under bruises, shame, and in some cases tangible dirt. That seems obvious and clear, but is often not so in the chaos of pain and manipulation. Discern their red flags. Do not fold them into a bouquet as I have, misnaming the taking of your love as love in return. Cherish something that cherishes you, and know safety is in no way a luxury here in our part of the world.

If you already know me personally, chances are you have a glimpse of my past. You also know I am alive. Not everyone in the town that helped cover up so much is so well informed, as the newspaper stated I died in my front yard almost ten years ago. Besides my obvious answer God saved me, I am physically functioning because I slipped and fell. Not because my husband did not want to hurt me. Not because he was not intentionally aiming to end my breathing. Purely because I accidentally toppled down on damp grass at the opportune millisecond, exemplifying God's grace through my divinely gifted ungracefulness.

Since we now have clarity that I am not changing the term "ghostwriting" to some new life-after experience, let me help catch you up to that point. At eighteen, I married a strapping young military man whose profession involved carrying cuffs as part of his day-in and day-out routine. His career, in combination with coming from a Christian home, gave him added perks in my mind. My subconscious implications propped him up on the narrow path disregarding actuality. I was aware marriage took dedicated diligence, perhaps even to a greater extent in one involving the requirements of living the American Dream, inclusive of but not limited to deployments. Having been exposed to some unpretty incidences from others' circumstances, I had acquired the understanding of hurtful lashing and mean verbiage; these are actions some individuals select to blow off steam. I never learned that it was acceptable to walk away. Before my recollection, my mother demonstrated this strength, in part to protect us both, but while maturing I did not observe life interactions exhibiting this dynamism up close by others, including those of religious relations. Couples rotted instead of healthily dissipating.

Looking back, I do not think I viewed all mistreatment as just that, mistreatment, but as human retorts to a messy existence. From my naive perception, I genuinely did not comprehend a defensible reason to terminate nuptials. Love was meant to joyfully approach the testings of our grace-giving abilities, able to conquer all. In its name, I risked my life over and over again.

Barely a legal adult, I was buying into being with The One, every parcel of my self intended for him, only and always. When he would press my comfort zone, I was pleasing my husband. When he would deceive, I did not rush to find out how many layers hid ready to despise. When I would have injuries to conceal and blood to clean, I tried to do so without complaint. I would fight when not allotted a few minutes to get a grip on my distraughtness, gasping to be heard, as if something I might say could halt his rage. This went on in one way or another for more than two years. Some people knew fragments of our dreary escapades, brushing them off as predictable in "new love," obviously we would have obstacles to traverse.

He asked me to quit a more than full-paid ride to college, dangling bribery of planning our perfect picture moment to replace our dismal hidden-chapel exchange. I deferred the semester. By the time he inadvertently demanded I stay safely home since he was in danger for our future freedom, I felt no room to argue. I did not see it as isolating or controlling back then. I was wrong! I thought whatever increased ease and reduced stress for him would be best for us. Meanwhile, I kept scrounging to force some semblance of a life from the scraps left for me. Here is my tender reminder to you: We all only have this one life. Scraps are not enough for a dog, and, by damn, they are not near enough for us.

This man had a greedy child's lengthy Christmas list of offenses he had committed toward me. He evaded experiencing any concrete repercussions while carrying on "above the law." It seemed not to matter who was privy to the limited details I found a way to voice or what anyone had witnessed, such as me being strangled with a gun to my head mere feet away from several men. Clueless to the fact "bro code among heroes" would hold so inviolable, I was appalled how people casually avoided involvement past this alarming episode's conclusion. No follow up check-ins came. Maybe they saw themselves in him, leaving it facile to take him at his word "it was a one-off." Whatever the case, apparently I disappeared out of thought while they kept down their merry lane. I guess saving a life is not what many people desire to spend their energy on, at least not those I knew back then.

This man taught me how to take a hit, instead of flirtatiously hitting on me. The lessons continued: enduring rib kicks from combat boots; people will avoid taking notice if you do not boldly vocalize your needs; you can lose your house, vehicle, income, friendships, education, and even church if you let the wrong person control too much of you. Did you know some states do not force inmates to attend divorce court? I had to learn that too. His teeth stayed legally sunk in for two additional years.

I could divulge page after page of miserably saddening altercations from this hot-headed, uncaring creature; but whatever drew you to picking up this book, along with the other stories entwined, I believe you have a general idea at minimum what people, statistically more often women, find ways to tolerate in the name of love and then fear.

I saw my strength back then, albeit mostly in the wrong ways: abundant attempts for show to cloak my incessant grappling with severe PTSD he had inflicted. These outcries, made while I lacked a solid support system, led to a multitude of destructive decisions chosen in desperate need to dull the pain, drown out the night terrors, and forget what he felt like on my skin. (This admission used to bring about immeasurable shame, not only from myself but a number of people I tried to get close to piled it on as well; survival is not shameful. Self-harm on the other hand in any way is dangerous to our beings.) Follow a medley of bad romances, including someone who later killed himself, and I met Mr. Two a.k.a. Trouble. The details to come are currently known by few. I will stay here with you awhile, uncoiling this second devastation.

Trouble was not the type to snatch my curiosity, except for his redheadedness. He clearly was not always found on the "good guy" side of things. He exuded sadness. This was evident at our first encounter despite the lively festivities we were plunged into. My nurturing instinct to mend was entranced from our first dance. With his artistically bad, obnoxiously bold, brutally blunt arm tattoo, I felt as if he was, if nothing else, honest. I yearned for honesty over really anything else at this point, as I had begun to suspect it was something only I could give. He also was broken, similar to myself. We could be comfortably broken together and repair our way to a content-enough future at least…maybe.

Our lives interweaved rapidly month one. Noticeably, our moral standings were commonly shaken on account of his recurring, seemingly random, scuzzy actions. We got married quickly with stunning picture proof. It was not all the love story desires that I now believe everyone should strive for. Our commitment was reinforced by individual desperations. This was a subsequent union for each of us, elevating the pressure not to fail. From the start babies were off the table; "medically impossible" I was told thanks to Mr. One. I wanted a life not alone with someone willing to adventure on whims. I could tolerate rough edges and grow a deeper love past the attraction of not being in solitary pain. Ending the first year, we impromptu picked up for a cross-country relocation to beachfront Nowhere he found courtesy of Craigslist. He became my best friend and regularly only one in proximity.

By this point, at twenty-four, I knew being pummeled was not okay. I unfortunately was STILL uncertain whether I would permit it when push came to shove. Beneficial to my unsure self, this was not his fancy. In exchange, the head games seeped in. Having already impelled me to give up the life I previously salvaged piece by piece, he kept me on my toes. Whilst playing my unsolicited savior, he confined us within his downward spiral of misery. Being removed from him for some time now, I can clearly see his typical conduct was ordinarily for sport.

Our home was not healthy, but social media looked as if we were chasing dreams on a struggling budget where passions can fuel more than just cars. We both had medical ailments, but his became the primary focus of us. He received a lifelong pension as a result of our combined efforts and persistence, paired with factual wounds and audacious sprinkled-in falsifications he crafted to "beat the system once more." In the aftermath, my hurts and needs stayed in second place. His were verified, keeping us afloat. Mine were left forgotten except by me unless flaring up, then emerging as an inconvenience.

I spent full consecutive days with my best friend following the first year of being married. Sounds more ideal than in reality. I was hindered from seizing any opportunities to work away from him in durations of more than a couple hours here or there for brief client photography sessions. I adapted with work-from-home jobs, such as online sales, and endeavoring to be the best viable wife. All in all, he qualified for a caregiver so there I was, giving care while being bulldozed over. With these limitations came availability for exciting new types of isolation. We spent a large block of time abroad. Traveling the globe made it almost seem worth the emotional cost of perpetually fighting on our soaring total of foreign lands.

Upon returning, we purchased a house to make into a home. It was filled with yelling, tears, and torment prior to decor. I would not dare say all these shouts and harsh words went one way. By then we were in a bogged down cycle, but he seemed to thrive off disrupting my seldom found peace. There was no amount of couples retreats, support groups, or begging for counseling that ever gave true relief to this dysfunctional loop. The pattern grew, physical love had fizzled out long before, and now we stayed haphazardly, intoxicated with weariness as he manufactured mayhem.

Our indebtedness was on incline. If I made plans for myself, even those to mitigate our mounting bills, cancellation was inevitable due to anxiety and puffy eyes from prolonged tears. Our last couple years I spent major time crying in bed. Not alone, not wallowing, but begging for it all to pause. He would stand in the doorway of our small room, implying a feeling of captivity, and keep the fights going for hours until the day was done. My eyes would reach the point they could not shed another single tear, and one of countless meals would go without my partaking. He no longer would pretend to be a good guy behind closed doors. He was not nice, and outside interactions were when his limited charm was revealed.

By then, I had reached the point my whole life was outweighing what I could endure. I came clean with him on where I was emotionally: with everything going on, I was on the verge of losing grip and knew considering taking my life was not far off. In spite of my graveness I gave him a two month deadline, conceding to enable finishing out the year "regularly," before I intended to necessitate things for me, even common decency.

Those months came and went with minimal improvement. My wellbeing felt discarded by him, as if I was a problem he wanted to be rid of. I did take time for myself beginning the New Year by spending weeks on the couch clinically depressed out of my mind. It is heartbreaking today for me to fully realize I was living a life in which these measures were viewed as well enough. How could I have interpreted that as something for myself? I was not taking care of me; I do not even think I knew how. My competency in taking care of others regularly backfired. Out of everything I have withstood, this I consider my lowest point. I lost my spark to survive, and I was wrapped up in the rest of a plot I was not prepared to engage.

I would love to tell you now that I did not stay, I did not sickeningly over give, I got my shit and walked away, but no, not then either. My boundaries, where I could muster putting them, were exceedingly malleable. In the background, my husband was establishing a pretty reckless addiction to prescriptions. He was incessantly lying to me, but I was tired. To my bafflement, this developed more liberally than his recurring constant drinking, for which he sought a long duration of help to win me over in staying years back. I could not keep fighting it or him, so I let him continue sliding by, dispensing his never ending inaccurate tales.

I did manage to find him a veterans program volunteering to aid his various turmoils. On the day we prepped his intake paperwork, because, of course I was the one filling it all out, he heartlessly told me how he was yoyoing antidepressants and over taking other medications behind my back for months. It was as if he forgot about his insistent claims to me week-in and week-out of being free from misuse the whole time. Judging by his carefree blanked expression, he acknowledged no problems in this familiar enough unraveling.

The day he accepted admittance into this institute, which dropped the ball grossly by not verifying any details of his exaggerations to full-on pretend, was my birthday. This date overwhelmingly lined right up with a dire mental health clash of my mother's who was alone back in our house. I found myself disoriented, too many fires in need of juggling and no knack to do so. I feel as if not celebrating me, without my pleading, was the norm throughout the later duration of our marriage. Therefore, I should not have been so shocked at the calendar day everything broke down. As it stands, I have not seen or heard him speak since, with the exception of court proceedings and a mandated property exchange. All of my calls round-the-clock were rejected.

He never came home. Meanwhile, behind the scenes, there was theft, in the tens of thousands range, of funds from both my mother and myself. Of course, he lied. He kept me on hold daily, awaiting his promised calls. I tried to communicate via text almost nonstop for his four inpatient months. This was the only occasional avenue of reply.

In truth, by then, I did not want him home. I did not want to be giving him more of myself, but I cared for him. There was an overhanging, longstanding, fed by him, misconception of our friendship's soundness, to his favor. Based on plenteous prior discussions, we mutually deemed our marriage's success irrelevant to our continuance of familiarity. Pact Us would forever remain intact. I kept up my side, still trying every way I could think of to be a true friend. I did not trash talk him to the Tinder women following up on his lies or those who took false privilege to harass me. I only reached out to his family one time over this state of crumbling. My inclusive interaction venture was confronted by boldface, almost comical, lies: just another non-loving reminder of where his habitual denial and low rating of family stemmed from. I kept maintaining our life responsibilities when given any means to do so. I was duped, under the impression reasonable adult separation and division was within reach. Be that as it may, I have no earthly idea why I persisted with assuming he could ever be mature in anything.

The last time I intimately saw my second husband he laughingly assaulted me. I did not call the police. For once, I craved to. I really ached to stand up for myself. The dilemma was, it would have kept him from the medical treatment. I can not hide the authentic heaps of hope I held for his personal betterment, finally obtainable with having a team working for his wellbeing instead of just me. I took the route of sacrificing further by not picking up the phone for assistance.

My bona fide optimism clung unwaveringly from the sidelines during his program's timetable, though disproved dreams compounded. All the former retreats and interactions in the world of disability we had participated in subtly spoke about how abuse of any type was unfavorable, but planted implications to expect such conduct "temporarily" by virtue of the added hurdles. He seemed to have a free behavioral pass from all the organizations since we were not encountering emergency status. Now, full swing on legal drugs with a surplus of misappropriated spending money, he was looking healthier due to rapid weight loss, putting on borderline schizophrenic multilife lies, leaving me to clean up behind him no differently.

The financial bleeding amplified as I underwent another year of legal predomination. With no minors and limited deficits this should have gone smoothly. To do so would have required two reasonable parties instead of just me by my lonesome. Debts more than doubled with his shady court tactics. I spared no effort or cost to negotiate on anything he wanted, in non-contested fashion the entire duration. I beseeched him to stick to his word, repaying at minimum his sole obligations. Never once did he broadcast a means to settle and cease. Obliging us both to lofty legal fees, he decided to drag court appointments out more than seven times, his appearance deemed by him regularly unnecessary, every one of which I was present despite being in complete emotional rubble. My angst swelled with the resemblances to my prior divorce, I found myself familiarly subjected to libel under-oath documentation and slandering, listening to someone openly state their wrongdoings directed at me. Despite all of this, barely a slap on the wrist was implemented for those past actions by virtue of Southern principles to commonly brush adversity under the rug.

He became the monster I am grateful is not my problem any longer. The stalking and extra ways of continually disrupting my daily life have seemed to stop for now. I truly hope it stays that way. As my therapist recently discussed, "Abusers do not typically stay hung up on those they abuse. Unlike the victim, who is marred in various directly personal ways by their abuser, an abuser repetitively seeks moving on to the next doling-out situation. Abuse is their methodology, internally acknowledged or not." We have also explored extensive talks about safety and how no one can predict crazy. I do retain some solace in my ex's need to fight, with my now long removal from the toxic relapses, I offer next to nothing in that domain. Putting this in print to you though did initially engender thoughts of concern I was not expecting. My story, My voice, My power is worth sharing.

I Imagine you are asking "Where is the good?" Inspiring others by revealing our paths to thriving after hardship is an enormous part of this book's message. My pragmatic grandiose outcome is intermittently still challenging for me to fathom.

I had someone do something for the first time, which was to genuinely call me out. By stepping in I suspect they saved my life. This might not have been in a physically harrowing, typically noticed way, but their action helped me to detect and change the potential wasting of decades to come. No fights were stopped mid-occurrence. I was not told I was wrong. No one actually stood in my way. However, this beautiful soul asked one simplistically direct question of me, after personally witnessing much of the tense insanity near the end: "How would you fix this?" I still remember the stomach churning answer I rattled off intuitively without hesitation. It did not contain the words of someone I was proud to become.

They sat with me through the early waiting, in the time of unwarranted chaotic infliction. I was not left devoid of solace while quite literally abandoned in a city away from home. I am beholden for this genuine friend finally doing what I wish so, so many would have found the courage to. Opening my story for you is my way of beginning repayment of this care with forward momentum.

Disastrous marital relationship two was dawdling its way out of my life completely, but a level I had not considered was ahead. I had to work on me. I had wrongly given everything of myself away. I was found once more limited on what daily comforts I may still have short term access to, and at almost thirty did not have a direction of paved success that was in progress. Oh, my drinking increased as a guise to self medicating early on. Mistakes were made searching for my bearings. Obstacles or not, my efforts remained concerted toward figuring out how prioritizing myself was intended to be.

I took on personal challenges, including a full year of daily photography. I put in work, then more work redirecting my energy in healthier manners, then, you guessed it, the work carried on. Plenty of days it felt as if there was no gain, but in total, glancing back even from where I am now, I find it hard to comprehend I could not see any of the accumulation close up along my journey. My blindness was partially due to such deep seeded doubts paired with not yet fully grasping it was my life. I finally get to relish living it.

I reached out to friends, even expanded that circle as part of accepting positivity into my realm. I crucially stretched myself by asking for help when it felt uncomfortable to display a need, specifically with court rides and not being alone during those heart crushing times. I attended support groups. Much gratitude is deserved by the very giving organization and wonderful guide who enabled the opportunity for me to complete a full life coaching trek. My ongoing pursuit of therapy evinces hope of closure. As I keep reaching out nonstop toward new opportunities, I find potential healing and growth in these assorted decisions. Recovering from abuse feels just like that, recovery. It is not always pretty and far from easy, but an amazing feeling to achieve. Sanity is a beautiful thing.

I have been finding elbow room to expand my education, and the excitement accompanying this I was not expecting. My geeky self is thrilled having a bookshelf overflowing with information I want to ingest next, and another displaying what I have diligently devoured this past year or so. I did not know I was missing the peaceful fulfillment these shelves boast. I no longer get pettily teased for reading or wanting to have my nose buried in a book. Preceding my newly found merriment, I could count on one hand the books I read in my last relationship (this equates to less books than years). It was another small way of controlling or demeaning I never noticed blanketed atop me. Risking sounding cliché, I was allowing oppression of my own education in both my marriages without much push back. This spotlights how oblivious I was about my misplaced desolate self love. I accepted being stunted and confined even in my mind. Now, used books have become one of my most cheering treasures. Our unique satisfaction flickers and effortless characteristics make us us. These are the first dominos to teeter into disarray when someone forces a storm upon our life.

With my depression struggles I sporadically find myself vacant of hope and joy even though life is on the up and up.

Sadness creeps its way into my dreams or thoughts periodically, and that is completely understandable. I can not wish to wash away my trials, if victorious in that feat how would I have become the woman I am now? Even in their limitations, I did acquire irreplaceably noteworthy memories. I aspire to lay all the remorseful endeavours aside to savor an unprejudiced recollection of the jovial occasions.

My newfound self care has not magically knocked down the walls I passively built up over the years. It appears harder to remove those blocks than they were to construct initially. I have frequently caught myself dazed from running smack into blockades I did not know existed while navigating what true connection and safety incompass. I feel bountifully protected by God's removal of my innate reaction to hike up my skirt and scurry away from those difficult interactions. I know tearing down the impediment, climbing over the monstrosity, or even just breaking miniscule chinks in it at first are all notable applications of energy geared toward reaching the barrier's better side. This is a rarity where the grass is promised to be greener.

I am astonished to thankfully be in a committed relationship. A dramatic pause is acceptable and almost expected here, but now moving on. I would not have considered this choice before. He is more balanced and mellow, though has opened to my playful adventure-seeking side. He does not just love me by word but helps cultivate a healthy environment that I can love myself in. Part of his safehaven goal includes not subjecting me to the sound of his voice raised in any form other than excitement. While not exempt from human faults, his flaws are almost precious and are readily met with action to correct the matter at hand. I have found myself awestruck at his patience, markedly in the moments mine has slipped away. There have been streams of tears for which he holds no responsibility, but his compassion freely intervenes to give comfort, proffering a chance of repair to those slivers of my battered spirit, a result I never imagined. I have my grumpy days, untrusting times, and inappropriate reactions ever and anon, but all that perversity is losing stride.

He believes in my abilities, more than I may put thought in whether I too believe them. I tend to be headstrong, rushing forward toward my intended purpose, without stopping to think if I can. He knows I will.

Both our minds are equipped with my newly acquired outlandish aspirations, but harder for me to grasp is his certitude to encompass them in our framework for future plans. Even in the instances my artsy method stalls, he woos me by uttering new visualizations for my talents he plans to incorporate into our life ahead. No longer stuck in the never ending loop of Cinderella, I am reminded at every turn I am worth far more than rubies. (Proverbs 31)

As I formulate how to close, we are all weathering a world health crisis together. There are many unknowns for each of us, but my silver lining is shining in my eyes with the unpredicted enlightenments from quarantine. After all my time spent in a myriad of torturous events, I had not dared envision peaceful harmony with someone around the clock. We surprisingly fashioned lockdown into a game involving how long we can avoid direct societal contact. The prizes to reap are our collection of invaluable silly memories inside this constricted utopia which we will revere in old age. Wow, what a difference safety, stability, and jollification fosters! The biggest shocker yet, even to my mother when told, is I have found pleasure in hugs, perchance even cuddling. I am oddly apprehensive to unabashedly admit that, as if my reputation or something is at stake. Physical touch, not even in my youngster years, has never been my language of love or one I understood much. You are welcome for this blushing proof of mine: the right person can open avenues of completeness to voids you may not have known existed.

I am not blind to the fact this could read as inflated praise to some new bloke, but with my heart vulnerably exposed, he is tenderly guiding me through lessons with each one of the previously mentioned points of admiration, almost creating a checklist of specific reminders you too deserve.

I thought I always liked myself. Confidence never felt to be an issue of mine, but with his presence, I have learned how to let it gain roots. I can see my purposes on this planet. Hope of having my own family has been gratefully returned to the table by a devoted doctor's care. One day, the painful lumps of my narrative will no longer prevail in my reality. As the blessings continue to become habitual, I catch sight of how profoundly close that day is.

I should have never stayed for all the calamity, but I did, and it is not forever damning. I have never been too broken or unworthy for love even when I refused to require it of or for myself. I may have sought after it in plenty of wrong methods, but I still have breath to change. At the start, loving myself, to my core, really loving me, was harder than being shot at and lied to, so much heavier than just giving all myself away to someone else. Love is keeping at least some of yourself and growing regularly, becoming better for everyone and everything around you. Love is not living in depletion, lonely amidst the critics. You are worth it. I am here cheering you on. It will be easier than the pains you have accumulated, even if you can not see an available way free, please give loving yourself a chance.

There was healing I intended to complete before letting my future in, however, I could not rebuff his resolve. Sublimely undertaking our mutual roles as Teammates changed the whole nine yards. He has been and continues to be indispensable for chunks of my self improvement. With his steadfastness and forgiveness, I know I do not have to remain stuck as the broken one, even though I was at our outset.

I am honored to be Harley Dree. I can be a woman with a painful past, allowed the ability to mend those tidbits. Concurrently, I have someone to tolerate my awful cheeky jokes, as I try to comprehend the truths I am being able to unfold. Finally my baggage has lightened to give space for the bliss ahead. Today I do not know those men who played villains in my past, or what they have become. The significant importance here is I am irrevocably not the girl who afforded them the chance to wreak havoc on my identity, at long last. This is my unfeigned wish for you too!

Sarah Mitchell

Sarah Mitchell was born in Ft Worth TX, shortly after birth moving to the Dallas side of DFW. After graduating from Rowlett High School, she joined the United States Air Force under the Texas Air National Guard. She was away for training for a little over a year, and returned to her home base for active duty orders for about 6 months. Shortly after, she was offered a position at a major class one railroad, which she decided to take. She balanced the monthly duty for Air National Guard and her civilian career at the railroad up until 2012, when she made the decision to be honorably discharged and focus on her family and railroad job.

She currently lives in Ft Worth TX with her son, Jeremiah and loving boyfriend Donny. Sarah Mitchell has two sisters, Julie and Mindy, and three nieces and nephews, Krystina, Natcher, and Mackey. She has a high school best friend who has been by her side through every trial and triumph, Tricia.

Sarah is currently attending Penn State World Campus going after her bachelor's degree in Organizational Leadership. She balances school with family, career, and everything in between so currently does not have a graduation year, but is getting closer every semester.

Sarah is very focused on making sure victims of domestic violence know that there is a way out, there is help on the other side, and the situation they are in, is not their final destination. Sarah is also focused on volunteering in her community to help veterans making sure they are set up for success in their life after the military.

Her faith in God Almighty has gotten her where she is to this day. She believes the power of prayer is the solution to any problem being faced, because when you have God as the foundation of life, you have such a strong building block. She attends the Landmark Sovereign Grace Baptist Church in Ft Worth TX where she was raised in, and her grandfather is the pastor.

Psalms 23:1-6: The Lord is my shepherd; I shall not want. He maketh me to lie down in green pastures: he leadeth me beside the still waters. He restoreth my soul: he leadeth me in the paths of righteousness for his name's sake. Yea, though I walk through the valley of the shadow of death, I will fear no evil: for thou art with me; thy rod and thy staff they comfort me. Thou preparest a table before me in the presence of mine enemies: thou anointest my head with oil; my cup runneth over. Surely goodness and mercy shall follow me all the days of my life: and I will dwell in the house of the Lord forever.

Victim To Survivor: How To Love Through The Trenches

Sarah Mitchell

June 22nd, 2018, is a day I will never forget. It started with Shane and I heading to the drop zone, as we were attending a large get together with our skydive friends out of town. They got to make a couple of jumps, but then we had some weather come in, so we all headed back to the campsite and started drinking. While drinking is never an excuse for physical abuse, it is often an instigator for it.

Let me back this up a bit and give you the big picture of Shane and I's relationship before hitting rock bottom. December 2016, Shane asked me out on a date, beginning the move of our friendship into a romantic relationship. Things moved so fast; I could barely keep up. He met my son in January, moved into our house in March, and love took us from there. In the beginning, things were beautiful. Everyone we were around, friends or family, could tell how smitten we were for each other. But often, when things are that deep, that fast, there's a catch.

It started with him digging into my past and trying to build false accusations about things I had done. This, of course, would start an argument between us. Things would get heated, he would go a day or so without talking to me, and eventually, I convinced myself I did something incorrectly, because it was all my fault, right? I was the root cause of all of our relationship problems. Every argument we had, came back to something I did or didn't do correctly. About 8 or 9 months in, it was almost weekly; he would threaten to leave me. Which always ended with me pleading him to stay, graveling at his feet. And he would always choose to stay, but not without making me feel like scum on the bottom of his shoe. A large red flag I wish I would have seen was on our 1-year anniversary. I spent a month making him a photo collage of our first year together, different trips we took, places we went, all kinds of things, and had it placed in a lovely frame to give to him. He planned out a trip to New York City for us to take over the weekend to see Phantom of the Opera on Broadway, something I had wanted to do forever. When I presented my present to him, he said, "This is nice, but I kind of hoped you would have spent more money on me, I mean, look at what I did for you." Right then and there, I should have seen that he was a materialistic narcissist who was just looking for his next victim. Hind sight is always 20/20 though, I hear.

Jump forward to his birthday weekend in June 2018, we went to an outdoor concert. We had a decent time, I thought, until I triggered him. He got super angry, and to be honest, to this day, I cannot recall what triggered him into this anger spell. He started yelling at me, with people all around, including a cop who was directing traffic. I started crying, which brought the attention of the police over. I knew this wasn't going to end right. Neither of us were drunk, but we were over the legal limit to drive, so we had to Uber back home instead. This was again one of the nights he threatened hard to leave me, and I fought him, begging. When we got home he locked himself in the restroom, and I was pleading with him, please don't go. I can't live without you, all the things we have to say to convince them we need them, right? He came barreling out of the bathroom and choked me up against the wall so hard I was seconds away from passing out. He let go. We went to bed. Waking up the following morning, went as usual, honestly. He woke up before me, made coffee. I started making breakfast. We sat down, and I asked him, what do you remember from last night? With a chuckle, he says, not much. I gave him a very brief synopsis of the evening, and he told me he had no recollection of choking me out, so I guess it didn't happen. Was I going crazy? Yes, probably. Again, all on me, right? Another red flag I disregarded and formed into being my fault.

Now, let's get back to where we started, June 22nd, 2018. After an afternoon of drinking, we were all a little toasty and getting ready to go down to the main campsite for dinner. Shane and I started fighting, and we started walking on the campground, away from people. Somehow, we made it back to our tent, and this is where I thought I would draw my last breath. For the sake of our readers, I will leave out the gory details. He beat me into an unconscious state, where I laid for an unknown amount of time. Our friends we were staying with came back to the site to check on us and found me lying unconscious, and him just watching time pass. If it was not for those people, our friends, I am quite honestly unsure if I would be here today. The following day was tough. I had to go to the local police station and give my side of what happened, my friends had to give their statements, and with that, I pressed charges. I let the legal system take it from there, but at that moment, I knew, for my sake, and especially for my son's sake, I had to be done. The same hands that once loved me tried to kill me. This was not a healthy relationship. There was no coming back from this.

After a 28-hour road trip back home, I embraced my family. I arrived at my sister's house, where she was waiting in the driveway and hugged me so tight, I knew somehow, someway, things would be ok. I then hugged my son while he looked at me, confused. You see, I was coming home from vacation, without Shane, with bruises on my eye, cheek, around my neck, leg, and other random spots. He could not comprehend what was happening. But one thing he did know, Mommy needed his love, his hugs, his forgiveness for letting this awful man into our lives. I had no idea what my next move was going to be, but I knew I had a great family, an AMAZING God, and a lot of healing to do.

The climb from rock bottom is a tough one, one you will never forget. It will leave you with scars, internal and external, nights you don't know if you can make it through to the next, and so much confusion. You will have days where you are not sure you can make it, but trust me on this, YOU CAN! Where do I start? What all do I need to do? Can't I just pass this part of the process and get directly to the recovery and healing? Ultimately, the answer is no. I knew there were legal things I needed to get into action. So, I made a checklist, because, to me, things were easier to complete when I took the emotion out of it and made it just a step in the process. I needed a protective order for myself and my family – I searched google for my local Family Law Office and started this initiative. It was hard because I had to continue telling everyone what happened. Every detail. I had to rip off whatever piece of scab was starting to build over those wounds and begin again. But I knew all of this was leading to more protection, so my family's life and mine could continue, in whatever this new normal would be. I always brought my sister with me, because she was my rock through all of this. So, if you take nothing else from this, find yourself a rock. This can be a friend, family member, counselor, pastor, whoever; you DO NOT have to do this alone. The hardest part of getting the protective order for me was going before the judge and having to look at the pictures that local authorities took of me the day after the event, and say yes, that is me in these pictures. Yes, this event happened. Yes, all the details you are reading are correct. Yes, I want a protective order from the man I thought my forever was with. I broke down. I cried so hard I was gasping for breath. But with one stamp from the judge, this step was complete. I was moving forward.

While at the family law offices, I saw a card for a Victim Advocate and decided to call her. I had done one of the hardest parts, but I knew I was just beginning my road to recovery, and I needed some help, guidance, hope. She pointed me to a local agency that helps women transition to that next phase of life after an abusive relationship, Safe Haven. The people there, the place, all of it, was a God-send. I called them, and they immediately brought me in for an intake. During this process, you have to fill out a 5-page questionnaire. This includes random questions about yourself, but the bulk of it is about the relationship you are coming out of. As I went through this, I felt so numb. How did I get here? How did I allow myself to get to this place? What did I do wrong? But still, I continued filling it out. When I was done, I chatted with the intake client representative about my answers. About ¼ of the way through, I realized something. I was in an abusive relationship this entire time. Verbal, mental, spiritual, all of that constitutes abuse too. But I didn't see it that way. An abusive relationship was when someone hits you, chokes you, wants to physically hurt you, right? No. It was at this moment; I knew the man I was with, never loved me. I was the next victim in his game. It was all part of the cycle of abuse. Honeymoon to blow up, and everything in between, described the last year and seven months of my life. And quite frankly, it ended there. No longer would he hold that control over me. No longer would he get the satisfaction of my tears, my defeats, my pain. Safe Haven connected me with a counselor. I was one who never really liked talking to someone one on one, so they offered me just to attend group counseling, and see how things went from there. The following week, as I was walking up to the doors of Safe Haven for group, I had so many feelings going through me. Pain, shame, sadness, guilt, but behind all of this, there was a sliver of hope. The hope of a new life for my son and I. So, I choked back tears, opened the door, and walked in. After I checked in, I went to the room where group was held. No one was there yet, I was early. By the time it started, there were four people, plus the counselor. She saw I was new, welcomed me and asked me a bit about myself.

Advised, there was no pressure to talk, but if I needed to, they were all there to listen. I smiled, nodded, then came the tears and word vomit. I took all the words in my head, formed them into sentences, told my story, and felt a sense of rawness fill the room. Never have I been the type of person to share such personal things with people I just met. But there was an energy in the room, a comfort if you will, that allowed me to feel safe to express anything on your mind. This was the beginning of my recovery. I set up individual counseling and went to group every week, sharing whatever phase of recovery I was in. The ladies helped me to understand that everything I was feeling was normal. They helped me answer questions like "This man just beat my face in, why do I still love him?" "When will the nightmares end?" "How do I get past the random flashbacks that happen during the day?" and so on. I do not know how I would have made it through without this group and without Safe Haven as an organization. My counselor helped me learn again, that I am worthy of love. That right then, in that phase of my journey, I had to repair myself, I had to heal.

As previously talked about, my sister played a crucial role in my recovery. She and her family gave my son and I a safe place to lay our head when nothing felt safe. She would stay up endless hours of the night with me just listening to me cry She would try to make sentences, but not always accomplishing, or just be with me because I was lonely. Her children helped my son only see what he needed to see that this man was a bad man. They played with my son and kept him occupied when I couldn't muster up the energy to get out of bed. About a month after the event happened, I gained enough courage to go back to my house and walk in. The first time was like walking into a foreign place I had never been before. I was already so deep in the growing and healing phase that none of this seemed like it was mine anymore. Where was I? Was this my home? Our home? As I walked around, memories flooded. Yes, it was our home. But no longer. This was my son and I's, and we will rebuild into it, our life, without Shane. I tried to stay the night there that first day. I failed miserably and showed back up to my sisters' door late that night, and without a breath, she took us in, yet again. It wasn't until a couple of weeks later that I felt ready to go into the house. I was ready to clear all of his things out and start fresh. When I did make that decision, I had my tribe with me: my sister, my two best friends, and myself. We packed everything and put it out for receiving. Just like that, I felt ready to be in MY house again. Yes, the walls were bare, things were missing, but I knew in no time at all, they would be filled with things my son and I wanted them to be filled with.

During the recovery phase, I had five people who pulled me through: my counselor, my two best friends, my son, and my sister. When life knocks you down on your kiester, its who is standing next to you pulling you up that you can count on and that was my tribe. I had days where I would fall right back into the mentality that everything was my fault. They had to remind me that I didn't make this decision, I didn't choose to be abused, Shane brought all of his actions on upon himself. I had days where I would wonder if I could ever trust or love again. They would tell me, yes, but I had to put in the work now, so I could be ready to receive it when it was there. I had days where flashbacks were nonstop and weeks where nightmares wouldn't end. My counselor had to remind me that if I didn't dedicate time to deal with the emotions properly, they would do just this and show up at the most inappropriate times. Day by day, week by week, month by month, I was transitioning through the recovery phases. Are there setbacks? HELL YES. Will you sometimes feel you are right back where you started? HELL YES. But you must remember and remind yourself, you are so far from where you were, queen. Feel the emotion, process it, and push forward to another tomorrow. Before even realizing it, I had made the transition from a Domestic Violence Abuse Victim to a Survivor. And you will too. But it takes hard work in the trenches, but girl, you have overcome so much, now it's time to focus that time and energy on YOU.

Is there love after abuse? Oh, this is my favorite part, as I was writing I couldn't wait to get to this part! YES, THERE IS!

And you are so worthy of it! January of this year, I decided to go on a cruise with a large group of friends, not knowing that one of them and I would gain such a connection with that we would start dating when we returned. I know what you're thinking. How in the world can she trust another man, after everything that happened? Because they are not all your past experiences. That's how. Quite honestly, I wasn't even looking for it, but when it's there, you can't ignore it! I was nervous, scared, and many other emotions, but most of all, hopeful. That sliver of hope I had at the beginning, walking into Safe Haven, had grown into a massive piece of me. I was optimistic that love had found its way back to me. I talked with my tribe, especially my counselor, who was SO excited and shared in every piece of happiness. But, she also taught me to stay guarded. She gave me guidelines of beginning this healthy relationship after everything I had been through. But most of all, one of the things she told me that stuck, "You are worthy of receiving this man's love, and you put the work in in the trenches of rebuilding yourself. You are ready to begin this new life." I have been honest in this new relationship about my past. I felt like I had to be because I never know what is going to be a trigger or not. When the time comes, you will have to decide what to share with the new beau or not, that is entirely up to you and how much comfort you have. Just know that if they are right for you, they will want to know, and help reassure you every day that you are worthy of their love. And now, later in 2020, I am writing this chapter as my boyfriend, and I travel home from a recent trip. He is choosing to drive, listening to classical music, so my mind and words can flow so that I can succeed in one of my goals and dreams. This is what love is supposed to feel like.

Last but certainly not least, in how I have gotten to the other side, is sharing my story, so others know there is hope on the other side. It is possible to make it without the person who is abusing you. You can do more than survive; you can thrive! I share my story on different forums, hoping that someone reading and needing to hear they are not alone, feels just that. Not alone. Because we are your tribe, we will build you up. We will help you transition from victim to survivor. There is help out there, and there is worthy love waiting for you on the other side, sister.

Alivia Ferreira

Email: ferreira.alivia@gmail.com

Instagram: thatmom_liv_

Facebook: Alivia Ferreira

Alivia Ferreira is a 23 year old woman who has always been outgoing and bubbly. She was born and raised in Nashua, New Hampshire for most of her childhood years and currently resides in Northern New Hampshire. She has one son named Brawk.

Growing up, Alivia lived in a household of 5 people. She lost her father, Tony Ferreira in 2015 from a heart attack, her mother (also known as her best friend), Michelle, lives close by. She has two older brothers, one a retired Army Veteran, Travis and her other brother is an intelligent gamer, Ryan.

Alivia went through the Nashua School District and graduated high school in 2014.

After Alivia graduated high school she wanted to experience different career options. She has a degree in Baking and Pastry as well as a Cosmetology license. Even though she holds multiple degrees she currently works as a Patient Care Coordinator for a top Orthopedics office in New Hampshire.

When she's not working she enjoys her explorations of book writing and this is her first official novel! Alivia's biggest hopes and dreams are to accomplish the happiest and healthiest lifestyle possible for her son, Brawk, and enjoying this journey called life with her love Tyler by her side.

Alivia wouldn't have come this far if it were not for all of her family and friends who supported her during her most difficult times. Alivia thanks her mother Michelle and boyfriend Tyler for being phenomenal support systems, for always listening and never closing her out through all the ups and downs and even to this day pushing her to write this book without a doubt of failure.

Alivia Ferreira

Roses are red, Violets are Blue. I'll make your life Hell; if you promise not to tell.

One swipe right was all it took for my world to flip upside down. I was 23 years old, young and single looking for love on a dating app. I know exactly what you're thinking, what was I thinking right? I had been single for so long I just wanted to feel what it was supposed to be like to be happy and so in love. I had talked to a few people here and there for months. Nobody was ever really serious and things didn't actually end up taking off with anyone from the app except for one guy named, Tyler, who took me out on a date to chilis but we just didn't actually click. We didn't quite feel a connection and decided we might just be better off as friends and remained in touch.

A few months had passed with no sign of hope. At this point I was honestly just looking for a friend or even a companion. Everything in my life was just so basic and routine all the time. I had truly wanted to try something different that gave me a little glimpse of happiness. I knew I didn't need love but this app just became something that I invested so much of my time into without really even noticing the effort. It was something that so easily kept me entertained in the comfort of my own home.

Then, one day; finally I met this man. In his profile picture was a tall, dark handsome man holding a largemouth bass by the river side on one sunny gorgeous day. His account made me laugh because it said he was almost 6' 5 inches tall and well, let me just explain that I am barely 5 foot tall. His name read Marcus across the screen. I thought to myself, "Oh lord he is handsome, there's no way this will ever go anywhere." All of a sudden a few days had passed by, things were still progressively working out actually really well.

We were talking everyday at this point over text and I thought for once, maybe this could really be something. We talked about the occasional hobbies our lives consisted of. What we did for work and things that interested us. We actually soon learned that we had so much in common. "Wow, is this really happening?" I questioned. We talked about our families and how he had a young son. I had told him that I had actually been told my whole life that the odds of me getting pregnant were close to impossible due to a brain defect that I grew up with. Everything was just going so smooth and nothing seemed to be complicated between the two of us.

A few weeks into talking he kept asking me to hangout, go out for dinner, go fishing, do this or that but I just couldn't get myself to that level. I had always been a laid back girl when it came to meeting new people and breaking out of my comfort zone was not easy. I'm just a girl from a city where nothing crazy really had ever happened. I was never the type to go out and do anything unordinary. Breaking the rules was never an option for myself. Drugs and alcohol had never caught my attention. I was more of the type to sit at home with the family and hangout.

My father had just recently passed a few years back and I was still picking up the pieces to try to find a little bit of normalcy. My mom was my absolute best friend and usually, she was the only one who I ever really did anything with besides one girl that I was forever friends with since we were about six years old. Her name was Ashley.

Ashley and I had been friends for so many years we kind of gained a level of respect for eachother where everything was basically always laid out on the table. We said things straight forward and how they were. Nothing ever needed to be hidden and quite frankly why did it matter? So of course, I bet you're thinking Ashley was the first one I had told about this man; but that wasn't true. I didn't need the attitude and negativity because I for once found someone who I began to soon think was the potential prince charming that her life lacked. So, I continued on with this cyber relationship if you will and enjoyed every moment of it. Actually, I didn't quite tell anyone about this man. This was something I wanted to feel out for myself before making any crazy choices.

We were steady almost a little over a month at this point with strong communication and I decided it was finally time I had a date with this man. Marcus didn't think it would ever happen. So that Friday he had invited me over to his house for dinner and a movie. I was so beyond nervous, I wanted to back out so bad but I had done that about 3 times already and I knew if I did it one more time I would've lost any real shot at whatever this was. I packed up a few things and got myself ready to head out that night. I did my hair and makeup. Makeup has always been something I have enjoyed and it seems to calm my anxiety too.

I wanted to make sure that someone knew where I was after all so I decided to tell Ashley that I was going out. I had given her all the details and exact address of where I would be along with access for her to track my location on my cell phone. Afterall, I knew that at least one person needed to know my exact location.

Let's just say; I woke up the next morning completely covered head to toe in bruises the size of almost softballs. I ended up leaving in the middle of the night because I just wasn't going to allow myself to go through something like that any longer. I felt like it was something from a movie.

Something you never actually think is real. But then, I was living it.

That night for the first time in my I slept in my car in a parking lot. I lived with some family at the time and there was no way that I could go home in the middle of the night. I was already living in someone else's life that I just had way more respect for them, then to come home and wake the dog and the whole household at 2am. To everyone else I was just the girl who lost her father and home. I couldn't believe I actually allowed myself to fall into this trap. How? How could I be in this predicament? I was disgusted in myself.

The next morning I woke up to multiple text messages from Marcus apologizing and saying how sorry he was. He thought everything was fine. He didn't think anything of the situation, like nothing had happened. He said his apology and thought everything would go back to normal. I couldn't do it. I was so lost, confused, ashamed. I didn't tell anyone,I didn't know what to do or how to cope. He had no idea where I lived but I questioned somehow he would find me. About 4 weeks had gone by and he continued to call and text me. I finally had answered and Marcus had asked to take me out to dinner. Asked to take me to a nice restaurant, to show me how things really should've gone. He kept telling me how I was so different. He wasn't used to having a smart, intelligent girl who actually had self respect for herself. He wanted to try this again to prove to me that he could be the gentlemen he had promised he was the whole time.

I thought about it so much. I played everything over and over in my head for days. I questioned why I couldn't be normal like other girls. Why couldn't I just hook up with any guy or why didn't I just smoke weed or drink like the rest of society? Was this why I couldn't ever keep friends or have a boyfriend who enjoyed me? Maybe it's me after all, I thought to myself. Maybe I have to try this again and have a different perspective on everything and Tell myself it's okay to go out on a limb and try something new.

So, I agreed to it. I said yes to meeting up for a second date. He was so delicate, so gentle and easy with everything he said and did. He opened the doors for me, paid for me and treated me completely different then the first time I had met this man. I found myself actually having a blast. The night had ended and everything was perfect. I felt so relieved and so happy that wow, this actually was a great night! I was so far up on cloud 9 that I didn't even stop myself to remember the bad. I didn't even question him a second after that date. We continued seeing each other here and there. We talked every single day all day long. We were becoming inseparable right before my eyes.

Then one day. I received a call after work. He asked me if I wanted to meet his son. I was taken by surprise. I didn't know what to think, we had a long pause of silence on the phone call. Now i'm sitting there on the phone thinking to myself, "Oh my gosh, meet his son? Me? Why me? I don't know anything about being around someone else's child in a relationship.' I replied, "Absolutely!" realizing how long the pause had been. He said, "Great! I'll see you soon and don't worry I'll grab pizza for us tonight."

That night I had ended up staying the night with the boys and we had a blast. It was such a wonderful night and I think all of us had a little bit of a sense of confusion. We didn't know why things were happening so well or how we even ended up so happy in this relationship that so quickly become our everyday lives. Everything was so natural, everyday was spent together like we had known each other for years. We just clicked. He was the peanutbutter to my jelly and I was the pepperoni to his pizza. We were living this life until one day I was at his house when his roommate informed us that they all had 30 days until they had to be out of the apartment due to the building being sold. Marcus panicked with this look that I had yet to see. I didn't know what to say or do. I didn't know how to help. I just sat there and let them all discuss this situation.

A few days went by and I received a text message that read:

"So I know this is crazy, but I feel like I have to ask you. I know that you haven't had a place to call home since your dad died and well, I have roughly 30 days to relocate myself. Don't think I'm crazy or anything but; what if we got a place together? We can go halves on everything. Just you and me. We'll find a nice two bedroom so that my son can have a room of his own. I mean we've literally spent the last 3 months together every single night almost."

My heart sank and all I thought was, "Oh my god, is this man crazy or is he right? Could this be it? Could I finally gain a home again? I had so much going on in life I could never save enough money for first months rent and a security deposit and keep up with bills on my own. Maybe this was my opportunity to build a life of happiness and stop jumping from home to home and living under everyone else's roofs."

I had given it a lot of thought. At this point my mom knew every detail. She knew every single thing that had happened to me since the very first day I had met this man. She thought I was absolutely crazy when I had told her this was something I was going to do. I was going to find a new apartment with this man that I had only been dating for about 3 months and yes now, sitting here typing this out for you to read, YES I KNOW HOW INSANE IT SOUNDS!

Before I knew it, it was moving day. Papers were signed. Money was handed over and OH YA! We had found ourselves the "perfect' 2 bedroom apartment in Manchester, NH. Well, Almost perfect. (There wasn't any laundry in our building so yes, I was about to become best friends with a laundry mat.) Things were really starting to look up. I was so content for the first time in years. We were so happy, we had dinner together at this kitchen table every night after work, bills were being paid, life was just really shining for us.

Then, week 3 hit and it was one friday night when Marcus decided to go to the liquor store after work and come home with a bottle. Well, that night was this first time Marcus assaulted me. I tried to tell him how uncomfortable I was feeling with his level of intoxication and well, he didn't like that too much. I was sitting on our love seat in the living room late that night when he decided to pick up one side of the coach and flip the couch over, throwing me onto the floor. I tried to get up and leave the room. I just didn't even bother at that point in trying to fix the situation. As I tried to get up he repeatedly decided to kick me while I was down on the ground. He said I was always so uptight and lame; that I never knew how to have fun. I was sobbing at this point trying to make my way out of our very tiny living room and for the life of me I just couldn't make it by this asshole. I tried so damn hard and finally I made it up onto my two feet. He then decided to pick up our glass lamp and throw it with all his force into the floor, shattering the lamp and taking a literal wooden chunk out of our floor. Glass scattered all over the floor and I tried to pass him. He said this was all my fault. I tried to pass him yet again when he threw me up against the wall. He continued running his mouth while i just sat there pressed up against the wall thinking to myself; "Oh shit, I really screwed up now." For his one last attempt to hurt me, he kneed me into the wall so hard I thought for certain my femur was broken. He then told me to get out of his face and go to bed.

That night I went to bed absolutely terrified for the real first time in my life. How could I have possibly gotten myself into this situation. I had actually fallen for it and mom was right. Do I call the police? Do I call mom? No, no I didn't do anything because this was my fault. I had trusted this man who I thought changed after the first night. I was the fool. I fell into this trap.

The morning soon came and I couldn't believe I was actually alive. I couldn't believe I had actually opened my eyes in the same bed next to this man. Shortly after I woke up he soon rolled over and said, "Good morning, how'd you sleep?" "Oh okay," I thought to myself. "So were we just gonna pretend that nothing had happened the previous night prior? Right, okay." I gave him quick short responses before he got up to cook up breakfast after offering to start the day off right. I soon made my way to the bathroom when I realized how bad my leg hurt. I didn't think I was going to be able to get up and make it out there. Once I got to the bathroom and pulled down my pants I had a huge melon sized bruise on my thigh with a solid egg.

This was my new life. This soon became my everyday and I couldn't figure out how I would possibly make it out of this alive. Months went by and one assault after another kept happening. I had called the police on him two times by our third month of living together. Once he was detained and taken into custody for choking me out while driving home from the laundry mat because I didn't want to bring him in MY VEHICLE to go pick up weed. He came straight home after being held for only one night after meeting bail. He apologized everytime; sometimes bringing roses' other times making a candle lit dinner. Yes, every single time I stayed.

A week or so had passed since this time of him arriving home. He decided to start looking through my phone and found some old text messages from before we had started dating. He had instantly assumed that I was cheating on him. He flipped out, throwing my phone into the wall so hard it instantly shattered and made a complete inprint in the wall right down to the studs. He repeatedly kept freaking out yelling at me throwing my phone around until it was literally in pieces. The next day I had to go spend $400 of my own money to fix this mess first thing in the morning because one, I knew my family would be freaking out if I didn't answer my phone and two because I wanted it replaced with no evidence for anyone to find out that he had gone insane again. After that day, a picture of his innocent son was placed over the hole in the wall like nothing ever had happened.

As you could assume all of these arrests ended up leading to a court hearing. Well I decided to go to this hearing to see what was going to happen. That day as the hearing began I soon learned that Marcus was not the person I was even close to thinking I knew. The judge started her spiel and began to speak and go over details of both parties, soon into this hearing she decided to go into his history and explain his charges for this time and how the outcome would be due to his history. The judge starts reading the thick section of papers off. Now, I have never in my life had a detention before let alone sat in a courtroom for assault charges. I'm listening and focusing only soon to comprehend that she is reading off almost what seemed like 3 full pages of a criminal record that I had no clue about. Nobody warned me of this. Not one of his family members or friends hinted anything to me prior to this hearing. I had no idea until that moment that I was dating a monster and that there was no way for me to get out of this. The judge continued to read of assault charges after assault charges, burglary, felony charges, theft, credit card scams, hotel room assaults. 'Oh my gosh,' I had thought to myself. "I wasn't the first girl he had treated like this. How many others were there?"

That night we discussed it and I found out more details. So, his son that was spending the weekends with us, that wasn't his only son. This man had yet ANOTHER son that he never once had mentioned before. Why? Might you be asking, Well I soon found out that this "son" of his was actually the child from the first woman he ever assaulted. She took it upon herself to file and take custody away from Marcus so that's why it was never brought to her. I was shocked. I didn't even know how this could possibly be real life. How was this MY new life? What did I get myself into? How was I ever going to make it out of this alive.

A few days later and just my luck I was extremely sick. So sick I didn't know what to do with myself. I had called my doctors and they insisted I be seen right away. I was so scared to go to the doctors. How was I going to hide my bruises? But there was no way I could continue being that sick. That night I was the last patient in the doctor's office when I was walking out and received a call from Marcus that we were having his son that weekend and they were going to have dinner ready for when I got home.

Well that night when I arrived home, I myself had a surprise for the boys. I was pregnant. Before going home I ran to Walmart and bought one of those car window signs that said, "baby on board." On my way I decided to call my mother because she knew I had the appointment. I didn't plan on telling her but as the conversation went on she somehow knew it right away. She guessed it and oh boy was she mad. I had never in my life felt like more of a disappointment then I did in that moment. I wanted to take it all back and I couldn't. I was told my whole entire life that I couldn't have kids due to a brain defect that I was born with. How? How did this possibly happen? The whole ride home she screamed at me. This was in some way my "miracle baby" and I had never ever wanted to tell my mother in that way. I wanted it to be special but it turned out to be the complete opposite. I just disappointed the number one-most important person in my life and I had to go home and act like everything was okay.

Clearly as you can assume my mother and Marcus never had gotten along from the first second they met. The first time they actually met was over a facetime call where my mom basically threatened his life and then of course he retaliated with absurd nonsense and I knew from that point on it was all downhill from there.

Finally, I had made it home. Right as dinner was ending I went and reached into my purse, pulled out the walmart bag and handed it to Marcus and his son. They opened the bag together and they were beyond ecstatic. I was still in complete shock. I was so confused, terrified and I knew that my mom was not happy with me. The boys were the happiest I had ever seen them.

This was my reality. This was my new life. From that point on I was in high dem,and fight or flight mode and I wasn't taking anymore shit from Marcus. I told myself I would protect this baby no matter what I had to do. From that day on, Marcus had laid his hands on me a few more times. Not as aggressive as previous times but still it shouldn't have been happening at all.

I quickly laid down some guidelines and Marcus soon learned that I wasn't playing anymore when I started to fight back and he started receiving marks from my self defence. That was his biggest pet peeve, any kind of marks left on his precious little face. So, what did that mean? At that point anytime he would come after me the first thing I would do is go for his face, I always clawed it nice and deep when I could get a hold of it. If, was the key word since I am so much shorter than him.

Things were really different in our relationship at this point. He was now on probation and I actually had a restraining order put in place when he was originally arrested.

At this point he was free on the streets because of bail and where do you think he went? Oh yes, of course he came straight home to me. Once he made it into the house I could never get him out. He always thought everything was perfect and just ducky all the time no matter how bad he did something.

So at this point I'm basically a hostage in my own home. I'm living two lives, lying to every single person I knew and well don't forget I was almost 16 weeks pregnant at this point. Later that week the worst assault yet had happened. We had his son that weekend. We were supposed to go to my grandparents for dinner on a sunday and the plan was to leave the house nice and early to spend the day painting and helping my family out. Well of course that morning Marcus wanted to be his arrogant self and fight with me and complain that he didn't want to leave until the afternoon because him and his son were playing video games on the couch. I said forget it, I'll just go alone. And before I knew it Marcus told his son to put the video game headphones on in the livingroom and he was booking it my way. He locked me in the bathroom while I was getting ready and pulled his usual shit. He ripped my blow dryer out of the wall, through everything all over the bathroom off of the counters, breaking the toothbrush holder and spilling the q-tips everywhere all over the place. I said it wasn't a big deal I was just going to go alone and he threw me up against the wall with his hand around my throat demanding that I wait so we could all go as a family. I kept trying to tell him to calm down and knock it off because his son was in the living room. I then managed to open the bathroom door and proceed to grab my purse and keys when he decided to come after me in a chokehold around the neck. He grabbed my purse and keys, throwing them in opposite directions. I tried to pick them up when he told me to get in his son's room pushing me telling me to knock it off. He threw me onto his son's bed then jumped on top of me choking me again while making his son's bed collapse. The bed falling made him get up off of me for a brief moment for me to catch my air and make it to my feet. Now remember I'm pregnant trying to fight my hardest against this asshole so I try to push him aside to make it out of the small room while ripping his shirt for slight distraction when he dragged me by my hair into the kitchen corner. He then grabbed my neck continuing to swear and yell at me. He then slammed me up against the pantry closet using all his force choking me. He started repeatedly slamming my head off the wall yelling at me. All that was running through my head was my brain defect and that he was literally trying to kill me. He picked me up off of the ground by my throat, I remember starting to see black feeling my toes just graze across the floor as he threw me into our bedroom slamming the door. He told me that if i kept acting like this that hed make sure I was dead and that if I died that he was going to kill this baby also. He kept repeating that he wanted to make sure that he put me in the hospital for a long time.

He came over again and got on top of me. I had a black hoody on and I just remember his knee continuing to push into my stomach harder and harder. I kept trying to get his face or claw his arms but I couldn't. I was so weak at this point. I could barely see, I couldn't breath and I thought for sure the baby was dead. While on top of me he started choking me again. This time I felt my body start to tingle, my lips started to go numb, my joints weren't working and everything turned black. All of a sudden I remembered that I had my phone in my pocket. I reached down and held the volume button and the power button setting the phone to call 911 emergency services. The phone sounded off a siren when he realized I had done something. He started screaming, grabbing his clothes, packing a bag and he picked up his son and flew out the back doors down the fire stairs. By the time he made it to the bottom of the stairs the house was already surrounded with police. His son was picked up by someone else, Marcus was taken to jail and I was evaluated by EMS.

I never fell for another one of his episodes. After this day he was detained and placed in jail for assault and strangulation charges while breaking a restraining order. He's serving 2 ½ to 5 years in Prison and he's missing out on the most amazing child that has ever been born. Yes, thankfully my son made it out alive. And oh yes, remember the beginning of my story when I mentioned that guys Tyler? The one who took me on a date to chilis? Yeah, well that man is the love of my life. He has been by my side every single day since. He was there for every moment of labor and he was there to pick up all the pieces after my life had shattered. Tyler is the most amazing father to my son, and I live every single day with my best friend. My mom and family absolutely adore him, and I plan on spending eternity with this man. He buys me flowers because he loves me; not because he beat me the day prior and needs to fill that gap. He cooks me dinner because we're a team, not because I'm a shitty cooker and can't do anything right. Tyler looks into my eyes and tells me he loves me because he does. Because we were meant to be a family. And most importantly he showed my son what real, loving, hardworking, caring man is supposed to be. And if you're wondering, yes my mom and I are still so close, closer than ever now that I have my son actually. And as for Ashley, we haven't talked at all since. This is the happiest I have ever been, and it feels amazing to be in a good place. I know my son will grow up to be an amazing man and we will raise him in this household what it means to be a gentleman.

In Closing

I encourage you to reach out and support survivors and domestic violence organizations that are working to help survivors. They are saving lives on a daily basis and need your support. If you are experiencing abuse please contact the national domestic violence hotline at 1-800-799-7233.

Made in the USA
Columbia, SC
17 July 2020